THE
PROO

THE NEIGHBOURS
PROGRAMME GUIDE

Josephine Monroe

First published in 1994 by
Virgin Books
an imprint of Virgin Publishing Ltd
332 Ladbroke Grove
London W10 5AH

Text copyright © Josephine Monroe, 1994
Neighbours TV series produced by Grundy Television

Typeset by CentraCet Ltd, Cambridge
Printed and bound by Cox & Wyman Ltd, Reading,
Berks.

ISBN 0 86369 831 X

CONTENTS

v

ACKNOWLEDGEMENTS

I would like to thank the following people for their help and patience during the writing of this book: Vicky Mayer, Joanne Higgs, Ally Oliver, and especially Emma Senyard. I would also like to thank Tiffany Jones at Grundy in London and Katrina Ray at Grundy in Australia.

INTRODUCTION

When Australians first said 'G'day' to *Neighbours* on 18 March 1985, no one watching could have guessed that they were witnessing the birth of a TV miracle.

Originally devised as a cheap 'filler' programme, *Neighbours* has grown to become Australia's most successful TV export – ever! With its simple values, mini-crises and harmless pranks it offends no one and entertains millions of people all over the world.

And nobody has been more surprised by its success than the show's original creators who described it as the 'What do we do now? show'!

However, although the basic idea of three very different families living in the same suburban street seems very simple, the formula that makes *Neighbours* work is actually a stroke of genius.

A little comedy, a little drama, and little of everything seems to be the perfect recipe, and every day at lunchtime and tea-time 15 million people in Britain tune in to sample the dish of the day.

Neighbours' success earned it a place in the history books when it became the first television programme ever in Australia to be axed and then picked up by a rival TV station. It made history again in Britain where it was the first drama ever to be shown five days a week.

1

Despite this groundbreaking success, *Neighbours* has been panned by critics. But the fans defy those who pretend to know better and continue to tune in to the show that has made international superstars of Kylie Minogue, Jason Donovan, Craig McLachlan and Scott Michaelson. Indeed, for almost all of the actors and actresses who have set foot in Ramsay Street, *Neighbours* has been a launch pad to greater things and the stars of the show regularly travel the globe making use of their stunning popularity.

But *Neighbours* has made its name in other ways too, and the preposterous nature of some of the storylines, and the reappearances of characters looking completely different after being recast has earned the show a kind of kitsch affection with a cult audience, and at universities throughout the land some of the brightest students in the country never fail to tune in. The soap also has a dedicated core of viewers of housewives and schoolkids who just thoroughly enjoy being entertained.

In 1994, the 2000th episode of *Neighbours* was screened in the UK notching up a formidable milestone in soap history. And as viewers continue to be enthralled by the domestic slanging matches and romances of those folk from Ramsay Street, it looks like we could be watching the 4000th episode in another eight years' time.

Neighbours has never pretended to be high-class drama but it has always been, and will continue to be, high-class entertainment.

THE STORY OF
SOAP SUCCESS

How It All Began

The task of creating the Australian supersoap was given to TV veteran Reg Watson, who had previously masterminded the hugely successful *Crossroads* in Britain. In Australia, he had made his name with shows like *Sons and Daughters*, *The Young Doctors* and *Prisoner*. But Reg had always had an idea for a show based on the Brisbane streets where he'd grown up.

Reg's inspiration came also from *Coronation Street*, the soap that had had him hooked during the years he lived in Britain (as well as *Crossroads*, Reg also worked on the old soap *Emergency Ward 10*, and numerous game shows), and it was the time that he'd spent in the UK that made him sure the show he was hatching would be perfect for the Poms too.

He finally got the chance to develop *Neighbours* in 1984 when he was head of TV Drama at the Grundy Organisation in Australia. Reg was so confident that the Brits would love his new soap that he had discussions about making *Neighbours* a co-production with the BBC, but the Corporation took so long in coming up with its daytime schedules that the deal was scrapped.

It was Ian Holmes, then head of production at Grundy (the company who make *Neighbours*) who made the decision to produce the soap without the Beeb's assistance, and it couldn't have been many years before the BBC regretted its slackness in getting its schedules together.

Reg was given the go-ahead to come up with the framework for the new show, but even though *Neighbours* had been in his mind for years, when it came to putting pen to paper it wasn't as easy as he'd anticipated.

The formula was simple – three very different families living on the same street sharing whirlwind romances, minor crises and a lot of laughs. However, the formula was so simple that Reg had difficulty capturing the right atmosphere and ended up writing twenty drafts of the first episode!

He had an equally tough time coming up with a name for his new show, and threw out the proposed options of *No Through Road* and *One Way Street* before settling on the title that it now so familiar that it's hard to imagine *Neighbours* being called anything else.

Following Grundy's recent flop soap *Possession*, Reg knew he had to make *Neighbours* a hit and a good way of assuring a large audience was to have characters that appealed to all ages. So Reg created the characters of Helen Daniels (in her sixties) and Lucy Robinson (only nine).

Another way to stop viewers reaching for the off button was to make sure that *Neighbours* didn't offend, and so Reg made an unwritten rule that the violence, sex and murder present in other shows would not be found in *Neighbours*.

Reg wanted viewers to say 'That could be me', 'That could be my street', so nothing was going to be too dangerous – a newspaper delivered to the wrong house was more likely to start an argument than an extra-marital fling.

But most importantly, *Neighbours* would have the one ingredient that was missing from so many other soaps – comedy. With three lighter storylines for every serious one, *Neighbours* promised viewers great entertainment.

The three families that Reg finally created were the Ramsays, the Robinsons and the Clarkes.

Max Ramsay was the typical Aussie beer-drinking larakin. He had a sense of humour, a quick temper and was a chauvinist. He bullied his sons, Shane and Danny, in what he thought was light-hearted bantering, and he adored his European wife, Maria. Ramsay Street had been named after his grandfather, and so consequently Max would be very bullish about the way things were done in 'his' street.

The Robinsons were what the British would call 'more middle class' (there is no class system in Ramsay Street, or indeed most of Australia). Jim Robinson, the forty-something head of the household was an engineer with his own firm, and his eldest son Paul was studying to follow in his father's footsteps.

Widower Jim also had three other children – Julie, Scott and Lucy. His wife Anne had died giving birth to Lucy, so Anne's mother, Helen Daniels, became housekeeper and confidante to the babbling brood.

The third family, the Clarkes, would take a little longer to come together, but the wheels were set in motion in the very first episode when Daphne Lawrence – the stripper at banker Des Clarke's stag night – became his lodger after he was jilted.

Once the characters had been formed, a budget for the first year of production was set at A\$8 million

– an incredibly low price – and Holmes started looking for a studio, and as there was space at their Nunawading studios in Melbourne, it was quickly chosen to be *Neighbours*' new home. It also meant that a 'Ramsay Street' had to be found nearby, and location scouts looked at every cul-de-sac in Melbourne in their quest! Several were selected for the short list, but in the end the producers settled on a quiet street called Pin Oak Court in the suburb of Vermont because it had plenty of rear access for filming in the gardens. The residents of The Court, as it is known, agreed to the filming for a modest remuneration (they were told that the show was a small affair that would only last a couple of years – 'It won't be too much of an inconvenience') and the next step was to audition for a cast.

They selected a mixture of established actors (Alan Dale of *Young Doctors* fame, and Anne Haddy from *Sons and Daughters*) and new faces (Peter O'Brien and David Clencie), who were all briefed by Reg before filming began. He told them he wanted colourful characters – the sort of people you'd like to have as your neighbours, rather than the sort of people who probably are.

Production finally started in January 1985 amid much secrecy so that rival channels didn't know what to expect (the soap had already been sold to Channel Seven) and finally, at 5.30 p.m. on 18 March the world had its first look at *Neighbours*.

But the optimism of the cast and crew soon dwindled – at approximately the same rate as the viewing figures. Something was wrong – but no one knew how to fix it.

UPS AND DOWNS

After just six months and only 171 episodes, Channel Seven announced that it was dropping *Neighbours* from its schedule.

The first to hear the unexpected news was Peter O'Brien who played Shane, who – quite by chance – was having a drink in the same bar as two Channel Seven executives from Sydney who had come to tell Grundy the news. 'They don't know it yet,' Peter overheard. 'But we've come to drop their show.'

Naturally Peter – who had been one of the few members of the cast to make a real impression on the viewers – was shocked, and the next day he contacted his producer to see if it was true – and it was.

The reasons behind the decision varied from the fact that Channel Seven already had two other soaps (*A Country Practice* and *Sons and Daughters*) to the fact that *Neighbours'* time slot of 5.30 p.m. meant the target audience of mums and kids still hadn't settled down after school (funnily enough, almost exactly the same slot in the UK was singled out as a reason for *Neighbours'* success).

But while the cast, fans and trade press absorbed the shock, Grundy's Ian Holmes was doing some fast talking that would make history. Ian was so convinced that the basic idea behind *Neighbours* was a formula for successful television, that he called rival station Channel Ten and offered the soap to them.

Channel Ten were so impressed by Holmes that they agreed to pick up the show – a television show had never swapped networks in Australia before – on the grounds that they could make a few changes.

First, *Neighbours* was going to have a prime time 7 p.m. slot, but Channel Ten also wanted to make some changes to the content of the soap. They wanted to inject more humour into the show – the idea was for it to have more of a sitcom feel – and they also wanted to change some of the cast.

It was an opportunity for those who wanted to leave to escape, and a chance for the bosses to dump the characters they felt weren't working.

David Clencie who had played teenager Danny Ramsay was one of the casualties, as was the actor who played Danny's best mate Scott, Darius Perkins. Both lads had earned a reputation for being difficult. While David refused to wear the clothes he was given for Danny, Darius made a habit of being late.

Darius was replaced as Scott by a relatively unknown actor called Jason Donovan. The two actors could not have looked more different, but the fans were so smitten with the 'new improved' version, that they didn't mind that Jason was blond and taller.

The changes in the Ramsay household also included the loss of bullish Max when the actor who played him, Francis Bell, made the fatal mistake of asking for more money.

Replacing him at Number 24 was his equally stubborn sister Madge Mitchell, actress Anne

Charleston, who was soon to be followed by her tearaway daughter Charlene, played by the little-known Kylie Minogue.

There were additions to the Clarke household too. First of all they found themselves with a lodger, troubled teenager Mike Young, and soon they were the first house in Ramsay Street to become home for the much loved labrador, Bouncer.

Naturally, the transition from channel to channel was not easy, but matters weren't helped when Channel Seven – angry at what they saw as Grundy's impudence in selling the show – refused to hand over the *Neighbours*' sets (the rumour was that they actually burnt them!), so Channel Ten had to spend extra money making near-replicas.

Channel Seven also caused problems by not screening the episodes they already had in the can in case it helped promote a rival channel's show. That meant a few readjustments for the viewers who noticed a bit of a glitch when the change-over happened.

However, the channel swap did have one very major advantage: the cast who were left behind had been brought closer by the uncertainty, and the new members of the team fitted in just fine.

And so *Neighbours* was relaunched at the 7 p.m. time slot a much happier and more professional show. However, the viewers still weren't tuning in, and in May 1986, the news came through that *Neighbours* was going to be axed for a second time. Even an expensive advertising campaign (including aircraft dragging banners in front of bathers on the beaches) hadn't been enough – it was doing even worse at 7 p.m. than it had done at 5.30 p.m.

But the promotions and publicity head at Channel

Ten, Brian Walsh, had a plan to save the soap – but he was given only six weeks to make it work.

Walsh identified one of the main reasons for the lower viewing figures was that people in Sydney – Australia's biggest city – weren't tuning in. Historically, there has always been a rivalry between Sydney and Melbourne – Australia's second city where *Neighbours* is made – and neither city likes a show to be set in the other. And even though, officially, Erinsborough was the suburb of a nameless city, the Sydneysiders gave it a name anyway – Melbourne.

Walsh used his A$500,000 budget to promote the show to take the cast to Sydney where they worked till they dropped signing autographs in shopping malls. Walsh also devised a competition for people to nominate their neighbours for 'Neighbour of The Year', and then arranged for the cast to deliver new TV sets personally to the winners.

The cast didn't complain because nobody wanted to see *Neighbours* disappear after they had all worked so hard on it. And it wasn't long before their faith was proved right – the ratings started to climb steadily, and the whole company was bolstered by the news that the BBC in Britain had bought the much improved show.

SUCCESS IN THE UK

October 27, 1986 was the start of a new era in British television – for the first time ever a soap was being shown five days a week.

Neighbours had been bought by the BBC as a cheap show to fill a couple of gaps in their new look daytime schedule. And cheap was certainly the word – they maximised the usefulness of *Neighbours* (which only cost a few thousand pounds per episode) by repeating each instalment every day.

Shown at 12.30 p.m. and repeated the next day at 9.05 a.m., *Neighbours* netted the expected audience of housewives and those people at home either through ill-health or unemployment.

But during the school holidays the figures rose dramatically as school kids became hooked by Des's pathetic attempts at wooing Daphne, and the revelation that Danny was not Max's son. And when term-time started again the unwilling pupils were so caught up in the events of Ramsay Street that many bunked off school to catch the show!

Those that did go to study would often sneak off in their lunch-hour to catch up with the Erinsborough gang. But it was one schoolgirl in particular who changed the fate of *Neighbours* and was responsible for turning it from a daytime afterthought to the BBC's most popular imported show ever.

The schoolgirl's name was Alison Grade, the teenage daughter of then BBC boss Michael Grade, who casually mentioned to her dad that her friends really liked the show. Her remarks set Michael Grade thinking – maybe it was time to take seriously the sackfuls of letters he'd received asking for *Neighbours* to be put on in the evenings so more people could see it.

And as soon as *Neighbours* settled into its new 5.35 p.m. slot (with a lunch-time repeat) it proved its worth by bringing in a staggering 15 million viewers making it at one time the UK's second most popular show behind *EastEnders* – and even beating the soap that had inspired it, *Coronation Street*.

With ratings like that, it wasn't long before the private lives of the *Neighbours* stars became the public property of the notorious British tabloid newspapers. The viewers also claimed the actors for themselves and inundated them with flattering fan mail. It was clear that *Neighbours* was more than just another Aussie import (Britain had already seen everything from *A Country Practice* to *The Sullivans*, but no other Australian show had created such a hoo-hah) – it was an *event*.

When a newspaper offered the prize of a visit to the *Neighbours* set, the editors were stunned by the overwhelming response – one million desperately hopeful entries in just three days!

Elaine Smith (Daphne) and Peter O'Brien (Shane) visited the UK for a romantic holiday (they had met and fallen in love on set) but found they never had a moment alone together. They were followed, pestered for autographs and mobbed when they visited the studios of the chat show, *Wogan*. British TV had never produced stars that were

14

greeted with such obsessive affection, and it wasn't long before cunning PR professionals saw the market in finding work for the *Neighbours* cast in Britain. Their names on a theatre production would guarantee a substantial run, and soon the UK was flooded with the Aussie stars cashing in on their fame during the Christmas panto season.

And it wasn't just theatre producers who realised their worth – record producers were quick to follow and offered the younger stars lucrative contracts.

The huge success of *Neighbours* had taken the British media by surprise, and people were left searching for the answer as to why the Poms loved *Neighbours* so much. Some said it was that the Aussie sun cheered up the British winters (and looking at the bronzed bodies didn't hurt either!), perhaps it was just that it offered something different to the British soap diet of unbelievable glitz (*Dallas* and *Dynasty*) and depressing realism (*Coronation Street* and *EastEnders*). Some claimed the early evening time slot made it irresistible to teenagers looking for an excuse to put off doing their homework, and some reckoned the timing of *Neighbours* was impeccable coming at a time when AIDS made people think again about family values. But few people admitted that the ratings were down to the original ingredients that Reg Watson had envisaged all along.

He was right – the Poms did love the humour, the classlessness, the lack of any real misery and the undemanding entertainment the show offered.

Neighbours-mania reached fever pitch as the romance hotted up between the most celebrated teen lovers since Romeo and Juliet, Ramsay Street's own Scott and Charlene.

The Robinsons and the Ramsays may not have

been arch enemies like the Montagues and Capulets, but they were nevertheless disapproving of how serious the two lovers were, at such a young age. However, the fans were more than approving – especially the teenagers – and actors Kylie Minogue and Jason Donovan became heroes for an emerging generation.

At around this time, a debut single was released in the UK with little fanfare. But the radio stations played it anyway as soon as they recognised the name of the artist on the record sleeve – Kylie Minogue.

It was the start of another era in British entertainment – it was to be the decade of the singing soap star with tiny Kylie leading the way. She really meant it when she sang those annoyingly catchy words, 'I Should Be So Lucky'!

KYLIE AND JASON

They were neighbours on screen, but they were also the ultimate boy and girl next door to millions of teenagers throughout Australia and Britain. Kylie and Jason were on the cover of countless magazines, and every day the newspapers carried another piece of tittle-tattle on the teenagers – the fans just couldn't get enough.

They were thrust into unexpected superstardom virtually overnight and every part of their private lives sadly became public knowledge.

Most of the speculation centred around the rumoured off-screen romance that mirrored the love affair of their hugely popular characters, Charlene Mitchell and Scott Robinson. While all the attention caused personal upset for the two stars, the attention turned *Neighbours* into a supersoap.

It was the show everyone was talking about, and their success paved the way for several other actors to follow in their musical footsteps, but no one ever emulated their incredible success.

Remarkably, both Kylie and Jason very nearly missed out on *Neighbours*, the show that proved to be their launch pad to international fame. Jason had originally been offered the part of Danny Ramsay when the show began, but the young lad had turned it down on the advice of his dad Terry (who later played Doug Willis in the Ramsay Street saga) who recommended that Jason finish his High School Certificate first. Thankfully, the casting directors remembered him a year later when they were recasting the role of Scott.

Kylie's place in Ramsay Street history came about by chance. Her initial contract to play tomboy Charlene was only for a week; however, when the producers realised that she had something special to offer they extended her role to a twelve-week contract. But before that had expired they signed up for as long as she would stay.

The reason for Kylie and Jason's success is not an easy thing to put your finger on. They are obviously both competent and engaging actors, but neither have yet come in the same class as Robert De Niro and Meryl Streep. And it's hard to imagine what their singing voices would sound like without being heavily produced. So what was it that earmarked them for stardom?

Well, their *Neighbours* storyline was certainly helpful – Scott and Charlene's wedding was the 'Wedding of the Year' wherever it was shown. People all over the world rooted for their young love to triumph over parental objections. And they were both helped enormously by the fact that British viewers were a year behind, so when Kylie left Australia in October 1987 to record with Stock, Aitken and Waterman in London, the single was recorded and released while Charlene was still on screen in the UK. Fans who couldn't get enough of the on-screen romance bought the single in droves, and the interest in the new singing sensation re-ignited people's interest in *Neighbours*. It was an upwards spiral that nobody could control.

Kylie's first single, 'I Should Be So Lucky', held the UK Number 1 spot for five weeks. Earlier in 1988, Kylie had already stamped her mark on the Australian entertainment industry by winning the Australian Rock Industry Award for the biggest selling single.

Just two weeks later, the then nineteen-year-old Kylie made history when she was awarded four Logies – the Australian equivalent of the Oscars – in one night, including the Gold Logie for Most Popular Television Personality.

(Jason also won a prestigious Logie that night, as Most Popular Actor on Television, and *Neighbours* itself picked up the award for Most Popular Drama Series.)

Kylie's success was so astounding that the Australian press even renamed the ceremony the Minogies! But while everyone else toasted her and partied until the wee small hours, Kylie returned to her hotel room where she collapsed in tears. It seemed the emotion and tension of the evening – coupled with exhaustion from overwork – had finally taken its toll on the tiny actress.

Thankfully, Kylie had her loving and supportive family to turn to. Her parents Ron and Carol were naturally very proud of their successful daughter, but they never pushed her into the limelight. They were used to having a well-known daughter, as Kylie's little sister Danielle (or Dannii as she is now known) had been a popular face on Aussie TV for some years thanks to the kids' show *Young Talent Time*. (Kylie also has a brother, Brendan, who is two years her junior.)

Kylie's collapse after the Logies added fuel to the speculation that she was anorexic, and when topless photos of Kylie (that had been taken while she was sunbathing with Jason in Bali) appeared in the press, fans were shocked by her painfully thin frame.

While the photos caused Kylie and Jason much distress, Kylie wasn't worried about her weight – she just happens to be built that way. The distress they felt was over renewed speculation that they were lovers in real life. Both denied the suggestion vigorously, although several years later they both separately conceded that they had indeed dated for four years!

The strain of such attention and pressure of a full filming schedule combined with the new musical career meant Kylie had to make a choice. And when her *Neighbours* contract came up for renewal, she decided to give singing her all. But just in case the bubble burst, Charlene wasn't killed off (she was packed off to Brisbane – Ramsay Heaven for most of the family) so she could always come back. The fans and producers always hoped she would, but her singing career took off in a big way and, as they say, the rest is history.

It wasn't long before Scott was following his screen wife off to Brisbane and Jason was chasing Kylie up the charts in real life.

His first single, 'Nothing Can Divide Us', was released in the UK in August 1988, and his first album, 'Ten Good Reasons', quickly became a best seller.

Scott and Charlene mania reached its peak in November 1988 when the love birds were married on UK screens, and the fans demanded that everyone's favourite couple record a single togther. The result was 'Especially For You', that year's Christmas Number 1 (to highlight the popularity of

Neighbours, Angry Angerson's 'Suddenly' – Scott and Charlene's wedding theme – was also in the British Top Ten).

Jason and Kylie's phenomenal chart achievements (Kylie became the first solo woman ever to top the charts with three consecutive singles) meant several of the co-stars they'd left behind also took their chances in the recording studio. Stefan Dennis released 'Don't It Make You Feel Good' with limited success, and subsequent singing hopefuls included The Blakeney Twins, Felice Arena, Craig McLachlan (who admittedly wrote his own songs) and Mark Stevens. Even Anne Charleston and Ian Smith released a Christmas ditty as Madge and Harold!

With all these soap actors jumping on the band wagon that Jason and Kylie had built, the two of them came in for criticism as they were banded in with their less successful friends.

Critics said that they were just riding on the back of their *Neighbours* success, and some even said that they were talentless and were nothing without the masterminds at Stock, Aitken and Waterman.

But they both later shrugged off the 'singing soap star' tag by going on to prove themelves in other fields. Kylie made the feature film, *The Delinquents*, which required the British Board of Film Classification to introduce the new '12' rating so Kylie's loyal fans could see it even though the star appeared topless in one scene.

And Jason finally confounded his critics when he took to the West End stage in the revival of *Joseph and His Amazing Technicolour Dreamcoat*, and proved once and for all that he really could sing.

Both Kylie and Jason were beset by scandal when

Kylie went for a raunchier image for her third album, and Jason took style magazine *The Face* to court over allegations that he was gay (he won the controversial libel action).

These events helped distance them from their squeaky-clean *Neighbours* image and it is rare that articles about these two ever mention their Ramsay Street roots any more, but fans of the show will never forget where they came from!

CRITICISM

Just like every soap before it, *Neighbours* took the bumpy road to success, and it had to endure untold knocks before – and after – it became a ratings winner.

Most of the criticism came in the form of digs about the 'banal' content of the show. People said that the plots were silly and unrealistic. Some viewers in the UK also thought it was unrealistic to have a man who owned his own engineering company (Jim Robinson) live next door to a self-employed plumber (Max Ramsay). It was soon explained to them that while these men may have made unusual neighbours in Britain, it was perfectly believable in suburban Australia.

TV watchdogs slammed the show as it failed to feature any racial minorities and tackled important issues in a trival manner. And parents voiced their concerns that children would rather stay home to watch *Neighbours* than go to school (one school in Aberdeenshire, Scotland, solved this problem by actually scheduling *Neighbours* into the timetable!).

Naturally, this sort of criticism came from people who didn't watch the soap! And even those who kicked up a fuss could still be found watching *Neighbours* on the sly!

Other shows picked up on the poor production

quality, the unimaginative sets and the standard of scripts and acting. But when you consider that *Neighbours* films nearly two and half hours of television a week – well over the standard length of a feature film – on only a fraction of the budget and in a fraction of the time, the endeavours of the dedicated *Neighbours* cast and crew are to be lauded.

To be fair though, it is easy to make fun out of *Neighbours* what with all the recasting of characters, long lost cousins turning up from nowhere and the comic nature of a lot of the storylines. But the light-heartedness is exactly what Reg Watson set out to create all those years ago!

However, the show has moved with the times and in recent years has dealt with teenage pregnancy, abortion, racism, adultery, as well as date rape. And when in 1993 the show came under the scrutiny of an Australian television executive, Bruce Gyngell, for being racist (he claimed the Poms only watched the show 'to get their quiet little racism fix' as *Neighbours* depicted an exclusively white neighbourhood), the show's producers responded by introducing a Chinese immigrant family, the Lims, and dealt with racism in an adult way.

Ironically, these sorts of 'harder' storylines upset viewers who had been happy on the diet of light entertainment that they'd come to expect from the show.

When Henry Ramsay and Bronwyn Davies lived together out of wedlock it provoked outrage from Aussie viewers who called Channel Ten to complain. It seems no matter what happens, there will always be someone somewhere who will enjoy complaining.

Neighbours also came in for some official cautioning. For instance, in the early days while the show was still with Channel Seven, it was censured by the Australian Broadcasting Complaints Authority for showing too many adults drinking alcohol! And in Britain, *Neighbours* created a real stink when rival soaps claimed its ratings figures were unfairly inflated by the lunchtime repeat.

As with most criticism, many of the accusations levelled at *Neighbours* were accompanied by the faint aroma of sour grapes. And as long as 15 million people continue to tune in every day in Britain alone, and Grundy continue to sell *Neighbours* to new countries (the current total is 29), the producers can take the criticism with a pinch of salt – the ratings are the only approval that really matters to them.

MEET THE NEIGHBOURS

THE ALESSIS

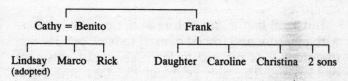

Cathy = Benito   Frank

Lindsay   Marco   Rick   Daughter   Caroline   Christina   2 sons
(adopted)

Identical twins Caroline and Christina Alessi were the daughters of a second generation Italian immigrant father. And like a lot of Italian families, theirs was a large brood.

They had an older sister and two younger brothers, but always Caroline and Chrissie were closer to each other than anyone else in their family. They were so close that they finished each other's sentences and often knew what the other was feeling – even if they were miles apart.

Like a lot of identical twins they enjoyed the usual jokes as kids – going to each other's lessons at school and fooling boyfriends – and although they always remained close, as they got older it was clear the two sisters were growing up to be very different women.

Caroline was naturally far more academic than her sister, and she excelled at school. Consequently, she became more confident than Christina who was less driven and more reserved than her twin.

Christina, it seemed, was destined for domestic bliss, whereas Caroline was going all out to excel in business. Caroline would always be seen in smart business suits, whereas Chrissie adopted a far more casual, girlie, dress sense.

It was Caroline's ambition that first brought the Alessis to Ramsay Street. In early 1990, Caroline applied for the job to be Paul's number two at Lassiter's, and it was a fairly straightforward appointment – especially as Paul fancied his new employee!

But Paul had learnt before about mixing business with pleasure and forced himself to back off. He was therefore very pleased to learn about the existence of Chrissie! The only problem was that both twins confided in each other that they both fancied him!

It was to be one of *Neighbours*' best ever love triangles, made even more tantalising for the viewers by the well-publicised real life romance between Stefan Dennis (Paul) and Gayle Blakeney (Chrissie), who ended up in a mirror relationship on screen.

Caroline wished her sister and her boss well, but there was always a little regret at what might have been if Caroline had got her claws into Paul first. Not that she had long to wallow in self-pity – there was a queue of men waiting to take her out. The first was neighbour Adam Willis who, as only a medical student, couldn't afford to take Caroline out on impressive dates. Instead he had to win her over with a sense of humour and incurable cuteness! It worked, and for a few months, Caroline enjoyed being driven around in Adam's beat-up VW beetle. However, in time, she realised she wanted a few more luxuries. And who better to provide them than a well-off, older man. Her choice of sugar-daddy was Jim Robinson.

Unsurprisingly, her boss Paul was not best pleased at the new relationship, but as neither Caroline nor Jim were taking it too seriously, they decided to ignore the gossips and the detractors and enjoy it while it lasted, which wasn't very long.

Caroline's ambitions inevitably interfered with her love life, and she often wondered if she would ever find a man who would not be intimidated by her success.

Chrissie, in turn, often felt patronised by her twin, who sometimes told her not to push herself in case she failed. 'I'm the one with the business brain, you're more artistic,' Caroline would say in an inadvertent put-down. However, Chrissie managed to persuade Paul to let her run the Lassiter's gift shop – which she did with surprising success.

When Paul proposed marriage and indicated his willingness to become a father again, Chrissie was ready to give up her job for love. At least she could be certain that there would be no surprises living with Paul – as he moved into Number 22 with the twins many months before.

So as Caroline got more and more business-like and spent more and more money on Chanel suits for the office, the only item of clothing Chrissie was worried about was her wedding dress.

Paul and Chrissie married in February 1992, and shortly after the ceremony Mr and Mrs Robinson announced that they were expecting. The news came as no surprise to Caroline who – sympathetically – had been having Chrissie's morning sickness and food cravings, and she had started to wish that she didn't have a twin!

But the telepathic bond between the sisters proved vital when Chrissie went into labour on her way to the shops. Caroline, back at home, had severe stomach cramps and recognised pains and alerted Paul and the hospital to Chrissie's condition.

Christina gave birth to baby Andrew and it seemed her happiness was complete. But, in true soap style, heartache was quick to follow.

The pressures of running Lassiter's and the Robinson Corporation were taking their toll on Paul, and his relationship with Jim had become very strained after his fisticuffs with half-brother Glen. It soon became clear that Paul was heading for a breakdown.

He had become too focused with work (at one point he nearly faced jail after filing a bogus insurance claim after a break-in at the office) and the threat of bankruptcy drove proud Paul to the brink and over the edge. Matters were made even worse when Caroline deserted the Robinson Corporation to work for Rosemary in New York.

Christina tried to understand and be a supportive wife, but she had the responsibility of taking care of Andrew, and now that depressed Paul was also behaving like a child, she found it exceedingly hard to cope.

Paul was finding the circumstances even tougher and packed his bags and left. Chrissie had no idea where her husband had gone, and she was scared that her son would grow up without a father. Lassiter's, meanwhile, was left in the hands of Martin Tyrell, a married man with whom Caroline was having an affair (she had been given her old job back by Paul after she had uncovered a plot to discredit him).

Caroline persuaded her twin that the best thing she could do for Paul was to hold the fort at Number 22, so that when he was ready to come home, Paul could start to rebuild his life.

It took a couple of months, but sure enough, Paul did find his way back to Ramsay Street, and he brought with him a big surprise for his wife. In tow was his six-year-old daughter Amy!

Paul had gone AWOL in New Zealand and had tracked down his long lost daughter. One thing his failure in business had taught him was that family was the most important thing – and he was determined that Amy should know her dad.

Chrissie wasn't quite so sure, but as it wasn't going to be long before Amy was shipped back to her mum in New Zealand, Chris did her best to welcome Amy into the family.

That family was about to have another addition arrive in Ramsay Street – the twins' cousin Marco. Good-looking Marco found he had an instant attraction with Beth Brennan, and although he managed to steal a kiss with her, he was frustrated that the romance went no further.

Marco's family ties were tested to the limit in the middle of 1993 when he discovered that Paul was cheating on Chrissie – with Caroline!

One night after Chrissie had thrown Paul out of their bedroom after yet another fight, Caroline found him on the sofa.

Paul and Caroline had become much closer in recent months and it was clear that Paul was finding it harder and harder to tell the twins apart when it came to emotional matters. So when Caroline went to cover the sofa-bound Paul with a blanket, she accidentally woke him and they shared a passionate kiss.

Caroline was so disgusted with herself for kissing her sister's husband that she didn't know what to do with herself. Confused, she avoided Christina and Paul for as long as possible. But finally Paul cornered her and said that they had to talk. Caroline replied that they didn't need to talk because she had already packed and was about to leave for Italy – for good. What Paul and Caroline didn't know was that Marco had overheard this conversation.

With few excuses and no reasons given, Caroline said a tearful goodbye to Melanie – with whom the twins had become great mates – and her sister, who was bemused to say the least at Caroline's sudden departure.

Marco was so upset to see Chrissie hurt that he threatened Paul that he would tell. But Paul reminded Marco that telling Chrissie would hurt her even more.

However, Christina didn't need telling as pretty soon she put the pieces of the jigsaw together and worked the truth out for herself and confronted Paul with her theory.

He couldn't deny it and he certainly couldn't explain it well enough for Chrissie to understand, and so she threw him out and refused to let him see Andrew.

Her stubbornness upset and angered Paul, but this time he couldn't bribe or sweet-talk his way round a problem; the only way to get Andrew back in his life was to make Chrissie forgive him.

It took time, but eventually Chrissie accepted that the affair had never been consummated and that Paul loved and wanted her more than anything in the world. He proved his love in a beautiful ceremony where they retook their wedding vows – and this time Chrissie knew that Paul really meant them.

They left for a new life in Hawaii in the middle of 1993, from where Paul would control the Robinson Corporation which he left in the capable – if over officious – hands of Chrissie's uncle Benito.

Benito Alessi, a second generation Italian immigrant and his Australian wife Cathy, moved into Number 22 after Paul's departure to be with their elder son Marco. It also meant they could keep an eye on their other son Rick who had recently been expelled from a private school and turned up on Marco's doorstep.

Benito was typically Italian – he wanted his sons to be real men, to be high achievers and to excel. So when it became clear that Marco would always be a good-natured drifter and not the business whizz-kid Ben had hoped for, all his ambition was then invested in Rick.

While his older brother gallivanted round the country, Rick was sent to a private school where Benito hoped that he would get the sort of education that would create a future captain of industry. But to Ben's disappointment, Rick too proved to be a poor academic with no inclination for business.

Rick rebelled and caused trouble at school. He was always behind the practical jokes that the pupils loved but the teachers dreaded, and, much to Benito's shame, Rick was eventually expelled.

He came to live in Ramsay Street and was enrolled at Erinsborough High where he became the instant bête noir of principal Dorothy Burke, before he found out that she lived across the street and started to behave himself!

But despite all the grief that her sons gave her, Cathy announced that she was feeling broody. Being around the pregnant Phoebe had put her in the mood for being a mum again, and she pressurised Benito into considering having another child. Ben hoped that her maternal craving would pass, but when it didn't he was forced to reveal that he'd had a vasectomy operation many years before.

Cathy was also forced into an admission – that her craving came in part from the regrets she had at having given up their first child for adoption.

When she was just sixteen, Cathy had given birth to a daughter. As both Cathy and Benito were very young and as they both came from 'respectable' families, she had been persuaded to give her little girl away for adoption. But not a day had gone by since that she hadn't wondered about their daughter.

The revelation that he was not their eldest child weighed heavily on Marco's mind, and when the rest of the family agreed to put the news behind them, Marco couldn't let the matter rest.

He started making secret phone calls behind his parents' backs in a bid to trace his long lost sister, Lindsay. When he finally tracked her down he wrote to her, but when she replied Lindsay made it quite clear that she didn't want anything to do with her natural family. Marco was deeply disappointed as he had anticipated an instant rapport with his sister.

However, his sleuthing had tapped a nerve in Lindsay and after a few weeks she could contain her curiosity no longer and she started trailing Marco.

She sat in the coffee shop watching her brother undetected because she looked so unlike her brothers. Where Marco and Rick had taken after Benito's Italian looks, Lindsay was blonde like her mother. Eventually, Marco realised that this woman was following him wherever he went and eventually he demanded an explanation.

When she revealed her true identity he was thrilled and insisted that she meet mum and dad. Lindsay wasn't quite so sure, and so they devised a plan whereby Marco would introduce Lindsay to Cathy and Ben as his girlfriend, giving her the chance to meet her parents anonymously.

However, the secret slipped out, creating an uneasy family reunion after so many years. Everyone was pleased that they had finally met, and both Cathy and Lindsay felt that they could now carry on with the rest of their lives. They agreed that there was little point continuing to see each other, but they did decide to keep up some contact.

Marco was also responsible for bringing his parents more joy when he started serving Cathy's spaghetti sauce in the coffee shop. The recipe had been passed down through generations of Alessis and had an authentic Italian tang.

It was so popular with his customers that Marco thought a sauce manufacturer might be interested in buying the recipe – and he was right!

The manufacturer offered Cathy lots of money for her secret sauce, but when they said they wanted to add a few preservatives and colourings she had second thoughts about the deal. Benito was also unsure at the idea of selling his family 'heirloom'. Eventually, a deal was struck giving the Alessis a very welcome and secure financial cushion.

Their younger son too was about to have his own dose of luck when, together with his girlfriend

Debbie Martin, Rick won a trip to London to see Michael Jackson in concert.

The teenagers knew there was no way their parents would let them take the trip together. It was hard enough getting the Martins and the Alessis to let them go to the cinema. But thankfully, Marco and Debbie's gran, Helen realised that this was too good an opportunity for them to give up, and so they devised a plan to get Rick and Debbie to London. Helen agreed to tell Julie and Philip (Debbie's parents) that she was taking Debbie into the Outback for a painting holiday, while Marco told his parents that he would take care of his little brother in Europe.

The truth was that Marco was desperate to leave Erinsborough – and Australia – because he was being hounded by loan sharks for repayments he couldn't afford. But the heavies followed Marco to London and when they applied the pressure Marco felt he had no option but to 'disappear'.

He left a note for his brother saying not to worry but he was never seen again, although he did make contact with his family to reassure them. Marco's disappearance was a godsend for Rick and Debbie as it meant there was one less pair of eyes to look out for them, and after Helen developed an ear infection and had to stay in bed, the teen lovers had London to themselves!

As they looked forward to seeing the Michael Jackson concert, Rick and Debbie had several adventures including meeting Terry, a boy fighting leukaemia. When they learnt how much Terry loved Michael Jackson, the Australians gladly let Terry take their place at the concert.

Their act of charity interested a TV show who

interviewed Rick and Debbie about their trip to London. But when the interview was shown on Australian TV, their 'secret' trip to London was uncovered by the Alessis and Martins who were fuming when the teenagers returned to Ramsay Street.

But the bans imposed on Rick and Debbie were to no avail – they were in love and nothing could keep them apart. And anyway, as they were in the same class at school, they saw each other every day.

Debbie and Rick got involved with the school radio, and Rick seized the opportunity to lampoon in front of an audience. Rick had become another in a long line of Ramsay Street jokers – he was behind every new scam, practical joke or misunderstanding. His on-screen pranks made him one of the most popular characters *Neighbours* had created for years, making the actor Dan Falzon a pin-up in girls' bedrooms all around the world.

So when Benito Alessi announced that the family was moving to Sydney in early 1994 (this was the first time *Neighbours* officially admitted it was a Melbourne show!), the viewers panicked that Rick – and Dan – were leaving the show.

Debbie was worried too that her boyfriend would be leaving town, and so while they were babysitting baby Hope Gottlieb they decided to show their love for each other by sleeping together.

But in their haste they forgot to use any protection and Debbie was worried that maybe she was pregnant. Rick, however, was thrilled at the new development in their relationship and resolved to stay in Erinsborough after his parents left for Sydney. He arranged an Austudy grant (an allowance for Australian school children living away from their parents) and lived at Lassiter's in exchange for working in the kitchens, and he presented his unsure parents with a *fait accompli*.

Ben and Cathy agreed to let him stay in Erinsborough alone when they left for Sydney in the April, and Rick and Debbie marvelled that now they had all the privacy they needed in Rick's room at Lassiter's.

However, their bliss was cut short when Debbie fell for Lassiter's chef Harvey Johnson and Rick called the whole thing off. He considered joining his parents in Sydney, but when Cathy arranged for Rick to stay with Lou Carpenter at Number 24, teenage female viewers heaved a sigh of relief that Rick, and of course Dan, was staying in Ramsay Street for a little while longer.

THE CARPENTERS

THE CARPENTER FAMILY TREE

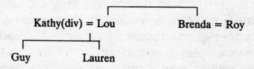

```
            ┌──────────────┐
  Kathy(div) = Lou       Brenda = Roy
  ┌─────────┴────┐
 Guy          Lauren
```

Lou Carpenter was a childhood sweetheart of Madge Ramsay when they grew up in Queensland, but he eventually lost her heart to Fred Mitchell and then to Harold Bishop.

So when Lou heard that Madge had divorced Fred and was about to tie the knot with Harold, he made the trip to Erinsborough to try and persuade Madge that he was really her ideal man.

And he had a lot to offer her. He was fun where Harold was reserved, outgoing where Harold was nervous but perhaps more importantly he was rich! A millionaire in fact. Lou had made his money as a second hand car salesman, but he soon learnt that money couldn't buy him love when Madge plumped for Harold.

The Carpenters next appeared in Ramsay Street four years later in 1992 when Madge and Harold rented Number 24 to Brenda Riley while they took a trip round Australia. Brenda told Madge she'd heard the house was available through the Queensland grapevine as she was in fact Lou Carpenter's little sister. Madge persuaded Brenda not to reveal her identity to Harold as the mention of Lou's name would cause him to have a fit.

When Madge and Harold left for their trip, Brenda's nephew Guy came to stay with her. Guy had become distant from his dad after Lou's divorce from his wife Kathy, and so his father was rarely mentioned. Guy and Brenda managed the Coffee Shop between them and amused themselves by romancing the neighbours. But while Guy's fling with Lucy Robinson was a rather half-hearted affair, Brenda's attempts at capturing Doug Willis had the precision of a military operation.

Neither Doug nor Pam were too worried by Brenda's overtures, as Pam knew her husband was an incurable flirt, and Doug assumed Brenda was just having a little fun. But she was serious, and Brenda also thought that Doug was serious about her.

When she realised she had made a fool of herself she was ready to pack her bags and leave town. But the arrival of her big brother Lou meant she would hang around a little longer.

Lou's first task was to make his peace with Guy, which eventually he did. But Lou had a much harder task just around the corner when Madge returned home from her trip after Harold's death.

Lou's old feelings for Madge were still there, but Madge didn't thank him for his attention so soon after losing Harold, and so she went away to Brisbane to be with her family to mourn.

However, on her return, Lou was determined to finally marry the girl he had always loved. But when he proposed over a romantic dinner, Madge politely turned him down. They remained friends while Madge made plans to leave town for good and Lou took over the running of Number 24.

Since his first appearance in the show, Lou had lost most of his money and it was therefore necessary for him to start his car selling business again, so he opened a car lot – Carpenter's Cars – in Erinsborough.

However, the recession meant the car lot wasn't the financial success Lou had hoped for, and he was forced to sell part of the business to Benito Alessi who was meant to be a silent partner. But when Benito lost his job at Lassiter's, he decided to sell some cars too.

The two men's sales styles clashed badly! Benito disapproved of Lou's sleazy ocker pitch, and Lou thought Benito was too gentlemanly to sell beers to a drunk!

Things got so bad between them that they ended up painting a white line down the centre of the car lot and agreeing to keep out of each other's way! Their childishness was hilarious, but nowhere near as funny as Lou's attempts to 'rejuvenate' himself.

After Madge left him, he celebrated his 50th birthday on his own and decided he was past it. So Lou resolved to become a born-again teenager. He started wearing tracksuits (none too attractive on his portly frame) and took up break dancing! And if that wasn't enough to put his back out he started dating Annalise Hartman, a busty, blonde temptress half his age.

He fell hook, line and sinker for the cunning Annalise who was really only after his money. Lou soon proposed and looked forward to his wedding night, but that was before Annalise's mother arrived and informed Lou that his consort was only seventeen!

Horrified, Lou called their affair to an abrupt end and his affection for Annalise turned into something more paternal than anything else.

But Lou was about to get a chance to really show his paternal side when his daughter Lauren rode her horse into Ramsay Street in December 1993. But the person who was most pleased to see Lauren was Brad Willis.

He had met Lauren a few days before on the beach while he had been surfing and she was out with her horse. There had been an instant attraction and they spoke briefly before she got back on her horse and rode away.

Brad hadn't even caught her name and thought he would never see her again. But he told himself it was probably for the best as he was already engaged to Beth Brennan, one of Lou's tenants at Number 24.

So when he saw Lauren in Ramsay Street his heart stopped dead. There was such an attraction between himself and Lauren that he knew it would be impossible to deny their passion.

As Lauren and Beth became close friends, Brad found it more and more unbearable to be in the same room with the two women in his life. But as Brad and Beth's wedding plans were being finalised, Brad and Lauren found themselves back on the beach where finally they made love.

Now that they had consummated their desire, they hoped they would be able to keep their hands off each other and Brad could mean his vows when he married Beth. But shortly before the wedding, Lauren had to tell Brad that she thought she was pregnant.

A visit to the doctor revealed that she wasn't pregnant but in fact suffering from chlamydia. Brad seemed almost disappointed when Lauren told him the facts as they no longer had an excuse to be together.

Lou, by now, knew all about Lauren's affair with Brad, but agreed to keep his daughter's secrets as the two of them were very close. All the years that Lauren had grown up without Lou after the breakdown of his marriage to Kathy, she had fantasised about how much better life would have been with her dad.

Her mum made her go to school and study hard, but every time she saw her dad things just seemed to be more fun. So she grew up wanting to please Lou, and that was one of the reasons that she started working with horses as she knew her dad was a keen rider.

However, Lou wasn't happy at Lauren's behaviour with Brad, especially as he had grown fond of Beth. So when Beth rumbled Brad's affair on the morning of their wedding, Lou was almost pleased that he no longer had to lie to Beth.

After the wedding that never was, Brad and Lauren continued to see each other in secret. But they were soon spotted together and at the risk of hurting Beth they started to date more openly.

Their relationship was never really going to work, and they soon learnt that physical attraction couldn't sustain their romance, and anyway, Lauren's horse, Chuckie Mental, was jealous of Brad! Chuckie was so important to Lauren – she had organised a syndicate to buy the race-horse to save him from the knacker's yard – that Brad was banned from going near the horse.

By the time they started to argue about Brad's gambling on the horses, it was never going to be long before Brad took a break from his relationship with Lauren and took a job on a cruise ship.

While he was away, Lauren met and fell in love with Connor Cleary. And although they had slept with each other, Lauren still felt duty bound to Brad and called things off with Connor. Her dad meanwhile was being a little luckier in love when wealthy Cheryl Starke decided to go after him.

She pestered Lou terribly, even buying two cars from him in one day just to talk to him, but Lou really wasn't all that interested. And when she proposed to him in July 1994 it was his chance to turn down a proposal – in some ways he was still just a little hung up on Madge, even after all that time.

THE CLARKES

THE CLARKE FAMILY TREE

Malcolm = Eileen   Allen = Tina Lawrence
| (div) | | (d.)
Sally Wells Des = Daphne
|
Jamie

Des Clarke had always been unlucky in love. Although Des was a caring and gentle man, women ran a mile whenever they met his mother!

Eileen was the mother-in-law that all those awful jokes were written about, and it was going to take a strong woman to stand up to her.

One of Des's early girlfriends was Julie Robinson, a fellow teller at the Pacific Bank. They had been due to marry, but he had tired of her nosiness, and she – no doubt – had grown weary of the ever-present vest that was visible under his shirt!

Des's next romance was with another Pacific employee, Lorraine Kingham. He quickly proposed and she accepted even though they both privately admitted that they didn't love each other.

But Des was so desperate to form the stable life that had been missing from his own childhood in Perth, that he wanted any woman to be his wife.

Lorraine realised her mistake just in time and jilted a dejected Des on the morning of the wedding. She went round to Number 28 to tell him the news herself, and when she found that the stripper from his buck's night had stayed over, Lorraine felt fully vindicated in her decision to ditch Des.

Ironically, this rejection would be the turning point in Des's life, as it meant he would need a lodger to help him with his mortgage. And as it happened the buck's night stripper needed a place to stay.

Her name was Daphne Lawrence and Des was instantly attracted to her. However, he felt coy about feeling that way about a stripper and tried to hide his desires.

But Des was so awkward around her that every time he tried to ask his lodger an innocent question, it came across as an embarrassing proposition. Remarkably though, Daphne was also attracted to Des and slowly they began to admit their true feelings for each other.

Daphne was the sort of girl that Des never dreamed of dating. Aside from the fact that their two professions couldn't be more different, she was gutsy where he was shy, wore bright clothes where he wore grey, was outrageous where he was introverted and was capable when he was useless. Des also knew that his mother would not approve!

There were several hiccups on their path to true love – and the arrival in Erinsborough of Des's ex-girlfriend from Perth, Andrea, was one of them. She brought her eight-year-old son Bradley with her, and informed Des that he was the little boy's father.

Des was shocked but happy to discover he was a dad, and he was going to do his damnedest to 'do the right thing'. He invited Andrea and Bradley to live with him, and although his relationship with Andrea remained platonic, Daphne still felt uncomfortable and moved in with Clive at Number 22.

Ironically, it was to be Eileen who would ultimately be responsible for bringing Des and Daphne back together, as she was the one who forced Andrea to admit that she had been conning Des because she needed the money – Des wasn't Bradley's father after all.

But Des had become so attached to the little fella that he didn't seem to mind. However, Andrea felt terribly guilty and made herself leave town – with Bradley in tow.

Kindly Des stayed in touch with little Brad and acted as a surrogate father, but now what Andrea was out of the picture, Daphne was suddenly interested again.

Daphne's wild and bright clothes and short, spiky hair were not what Eileen had envisaged for her beloved son, but when she saw how much the couple loved each other, even she was forced to give her consent to their impending nuptials.

But in typical Des fashion, those nuptials weren't to go to plan. His best man (and best mate) Paul got Des to the church on time, and it was left to Shane Ramsay (with whom Daphne had had a brief affair) to get the bride to the altar.

But the bridal party were running late because they were waiting for Danny Ramsay to return after delivering a gorilla-gram for Clive Gibbons' message service. But as it got closer and closer to the 'I do' deadline, Shane decided to leave without his little brother.

Luckily along the way they spotted a man running

in a gorilla suit, and as they assumed that it was Danny rushing back for the wedding, they insisted that he get in the car.

However, the passenger was not Danny – it was an armed bank raider in disguise who decided to take the bridal party hostage.

Des grew impatient as he waited at the church and as the time passed he was besieged by doubts. He told himself that he had never been good enough for Daphne, and he said he wasn't surprised that she had realised his uselessness too.

He was inconsolable and ran off, telling Paul and the rest of the congregation to leave him alone. He wandered off to be by himself, desolate and distraught.

By the time the bride and her entourage had rid themselves of their kidnapper, it was too late and Des was nowhere to be seen.

He was missing for days, embarrassed to come home in case the neighbours were laughing at him. But it was Des who laughed when he returned to Number 28, because Daff was waiting for him! They fell into each other's arms and made plans for wedding number two, which thankfully went off without a problem.

Daphne had long since left the stripping business behind her for something much more respectable. Her grandfather, Harry Henderson, had won the local Coffee Shop in a bet, and as he had no use for it himself, he gave it to his favourite granddaughter.

Apart from outrageous Harry, Daphne never mentioned her family, and it was clear that all had not been well at home. The mention of her father made her flinch, and consequently no one talked to her about her folks, and Daff's past remained a mystery to everyone including Des.

Consequently, Daphne took it upon herself to be a confidante to anyone in trouble, and she gained the respect and affection of the teenagers in Ramsay Street, most notably, that of Mike Young.

Mike was a local teenager who had been systematically beaten by her father since he was little. He had put up with the violence because he didn't dare leave his mum alone in the house with his evil dad David. But as Mike's HSC approached he knew he needed to make the break regardless, else he would never pass his exams.

His school friend Scott Robinson first brought him to Ramsay Street, and when Daff learnt of his problems she offered to become his legal guardian, and the tortured Mike moved into the Erinsborough cul-de-sac.

There was about to be another addition to the Clarke household – Daphne was finally pregnant! But it took Des's sympathetic pregnancy food cravings before Dr Clive diagnosed his wife's condition!

According to the actress who played Daphne, Elaine Smith, her character's pregnancy lasted well over the traditional nine months as the producers dragged out the gestation to tie in with other storylines.

In true soap style, the baby's arrival came at the most inopportune moment possible. Daphne and Des were taking a picnic with Jim Robinson and his latest lady friend, Beverly Marshall who thankfully was a doctor. But Jim and Beverly had wandered off and were nowhere to be seen. As Des tried to calm his wife (it was he who really needed calming down) he shouted pathetically for their companions.

Dr Bev arrived just in time to help Daphne produce a healthy baby boy. The Clarkes had trouble deciding on a name for their son. Eileen – who had come to 'help' – insisted that the child be called Kingsley, as it was a traditional name in her family, but Des and Daphne had other ideas.

In the end they plumped for Jamie, and Jim and Mike decided that the little boy had been named after both of them (James was Mike's middle name), but they were happy to put their good-natured argument to rest when they were both asked to be Jamie's godfathers.

Eileen's all-pervading presence in Des's life was so complete that few people stopped to realise that he never mentioned his father – but that was because his mummy wouldn't let him.

Malcolm Clarke had done the only thing a sane man could have done when he left Eileen years before. And as Des felt rejected by his father – he was only young when Malcolm shot through – he wasn't fussed about not having him in his life.

But when Jamie was born, Daphne wondered if perhaps Malcolm should know that he was a grandfather. And so he turned up on the doorstep of Number 28 and it wasn't long before he proposed to Eileen.

Des was thrilled at the thought of his parents re-marrying, but unfortunately it was not to be. The things that had infuriated them twenty years before hadn't changed, and shortly before the intended wedding, Malcolm shot through for the second time leaving Eileen with a wounded, if not broken, heart.

But real heartache was about to hit the Clarkes both off screen and on. The most devastating blow came when Myra de Groot who played Eileen was diagnosed as suffering from cancer.

Eileen may have been an old bat on screen, but in real life Myra was the most respected and loved member of the cast (Jason Donovan even dedicated his 1988 Silver Logie to her and her courage in her fight against the cancer).

But despite all the goodwill from cast mates and fans alike, Myra lost her battle just a few months after the Logies ceremony.

Des was about to endure an equally heartbreaking experience on screen too. Elaine Smith had decided the time was right for her to leave *Neighbours* and so she asked to be written out.

But as Daphne was such a popular character, the producers were loath to kill her off. So they invented a somewhat unbelievable storyline whereby Daff's long forgotten father – the reason for her childhood misery – came back into her life. But Allen Lawrence was terminally ill, and Daphne realised that she only had a short time to make her peace with her father. So she decided to leave Des taking Jamie with her in order to look after her ailing dad.

While she was away caring for her father, a mystery woman started trailing Des, and for a while the viewers were teased that Des would be tempted away from Daphne. But the mystery woman's interest in Des was not sexual. She later revealed herself to be Des's long lost half-sister, Sally Wells.

A result of one of Malcolm's numerous affairs, Eileen was not pleased to come face to face with Sally, but Des was thrilled to finally have a sibling, and Sal was quickly installed behind the counter in the Coffee Shop.

But there was only so long that the producers

could distract the viewers from Daphne's fate. They knew that there was no way two people as in love as Des and Daphne could bear to be apart for as long as they had been – and so the soap's bosses asked Elaine Smith to return for a few days in order to finish off Daphne's storyline.

The plot they invented was as follows: Daff's father finally died and on the way to the funeral she was involved in a car crash (Gail Robinson was also in the car). Daphne was critically injured and rushed to hospital. Gail, thankfully, suffered only minor injuries.

Des hung around the hospital for days as Daphne lingered in a coma which for the most part happened off screen so that Elaine Smith didn't have to hang around to film the scenes. Elaine was meanwhile being courted to return to Ramsay Street, and Daphne's coma endured for as long as there was any hope that Elaine might change her mind.

She didn't, and so Daff regained consciousness just long enough to say 'I love you Clarkey' before slipping away.

Des was gutted, but knew he had to keep things going for Jamie. When Mrs Kirkwood, the local babysitter, moved away from Ramsay Street, Des was forced to find a nanny for his son so that he could return to his manager's job at the bank.

The job was offered to Bronwyn Davies, a pretty country girl who had found Jamie alone in a shopping centre car park (the tot had run off when Des was grappling with his car keys, shopping, and baby buggy). She was not convinced that Des was a fit father after their first meeting, but he soon proved his worth to her.

Des's next love interest was his most unlikely yet,

and it seemed it was a last ditch effort on the part of the storyliners to give Des a plot following Daphne's death. Des was paired up with Mrs Mangel's granddaughter, Jane Harris.

Although everyone felt that Jane was mature beyond her years, it still seemed unlikely that she would fall for the hapless Des. But fall she did, and she made a very obvious play for the neighbourhood bank manager.

The couple got engaged, but perhaps they both felt that it wasn't quite right – it certainly didn't gel with the viewers – and so before the wedding, Jane decided to join her sick granny in England where she was living with her second husband.

Yet again Des had been deserted by the woman in his life. It seemed there was absolutely no danger of Jamie growing up to be a mummy's boy like his dad.

Disenchanted with Erinsborough, Des returned to his native Perth where he discovered a new trade as a stockbroker (he even had the sideburns and red braces to prove it on his return) thanks to a grossly exaggerated CV written by the wacky Melanie. But Des had found something much more important than a job on the West coast – love.

He had met a woman called Fiona who was also a single parent, and just as soon as he could sell the house he was going to move to Perth and start a new life with her. And so in 1990, Des headed west, and he took with him the heartfelt best wishes of all his neighbours in Ramsay Street.

THE GOTTLIEBS

THE GOTTLIEB FAMILY TREE

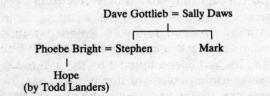

When Phoebe Bright met the man she would marry, Stephen Gottlieb, she was already six months pregnant by another man.

After an unlucky life in which her mother deserted her and her father died, academic Phoebe found she was pregnant at seventeen by her boyfriend Todd Landers. It had been a tough decision to make, but her legal guardian, Dorothy Burke, persuaded her that an abortion meant not sacrificing the rest of her life.

But while Phoebe and Dorothy were at the abortion clinic, word came through that Todd had been run over in a road accident just before Phoebe was due for her operation.

The two women rushed to Todd's bedside where Phoebe watched her love die from a massive heart attack. She knew then that she would keep the baby.

It was while she was mourning at Todd's graveside

that she first met Stephen. He was also visiting the cemetery as his fiancée Libby was buried there.

Stephen was instantly drawn to Phoebe. At first he just wanted to help her grieve, but then he realised the best way for both of them to get over their grief was to be together.

Within weeks he proposed to Phoebe, who surprised herself by accepting even though she knew she didn't love him. But she was young and needed his support with the baby on the way. But as it turned out, Phoebe and Stephen were quite well matched.

Like Phoebe, Stephen had also had a strained relationship with his parents. They had brought him and his elder brother Mark up on a hippy commune, and continued their alternative lifestyle in later life by joining a pub band and touring Australia in a caravan.

Stephen wasn't exactly ashamed of his parents, but he certainly wasn't proud of them. However, they instilled in him a love of music which proved useful when he became the manager of a record store in Anson's Corner.

Phoebe thought she was lucky to have found Stephen as she knew not many men would take on another man's child, but Stephen was so thrilled he seemed more expectant than Phoebe at times!

They made their preparations for their wedding which was due at the beginning of November. Everything was going smoothly until Stephen's stag night when he received a phone call to say Phoebe had gone into labour two months prematurely.

He rushed to the hospital to be with her, but their joy quickly turned to worry when it became clear that their daughter might be too frail to survive.

They aptly named her Hope, and indeed she did pull through, but that was by no means the end of their troubles.

Shortly after Hope's birth, Stephen became paranoid that Phoebe wouldn't marry him, and these feelings were exacerbated when visitors kept saying, 'Oh, doesn't she look like Todd.' Stephen knew it was going to be hard enough without being haunted by Phoebe's past.

He hastened their wedding plans and they tied the knot before Hope was well enough to leave hospital. Or so they thought! Their greatest wedding present was when local nurse Pam Willis arrived at the service carrying their tiny bundle of joy.

Married life was not to be a bed of roses for these two. First of all their great friend and mentor Dorothy Burke left town with young Toby Mangel to start a new life in the the country with Dorothy's new love Tom Merrick. This meant the Gottliebs had to take on the financial responsibility of Number 30 by themselves.

This was made harder when Stephen lost his job at the store after he refused to take bribes from record companies to falsify record sales.

Cathy Alessi offered them work in the Coffee Shop, but as they were both keen to stay at home and look after Hope, Stephen and Phoebe job shared at the Coffee Shop working alternate shifts. But even the money from there was not enough to keep their heads above water, and they were forced to advertise for a lodger.

When Russell Butler saw the card they put up on the Coffee Shop notice board, he was so sure they would want him to be their new lodger that he took their notice down and threw it away. If only Phoebe and Stephen had noticed that his behaviour was slightly unusual, then they would have saved themselves an awful lot of heartache.

Russell had recently left a drug rehabilitation centre where he had been staying after his girlfriend ran off and left him, taking their baby with her. Russell was so keen to find replacements for them, that Phoebe and Hope were too much of a temptation for him to stay away.

He moved into the Gottliebs' spare room at Number 30, and it wasn't long before this cuckoo was making Phoebe and Stephen feel very uncomfortable in their own nest.

His manner unsettled them as he told one thing to Stephen and another to Phoebe. He was very peculiar about Phoebe cleaning his room and flipped when he found she had been in there to vacuum without his permission. At one stage he even tried to kiss Phoebe, but still she was reluctant to throw him out.

Eventually, there came a time when the Gottliebs had made enough excuses for their unusual lodger, and after he had fitted a lock on his bedroom door, eaten their food and been unable to pay them rent they decided they had to evict him.

But Russell was stubborn and made it clear he would be difficult to remove. In the end, his bullying got to Phoebe and she took Hope away to stay with Dorothy, leaving Stephen to face out Russell in a head to head.

Russell's belligerence and meddling left Stephen with only one choice – violence. So when Lou told him that he knew of some heavies that could persuade Russell to leave, Stephen reluctantly asked Lou to arrange it.

The night the biker gang arrived to see to Russell they found Wayne at Number 30, but didn't believe him when he told them they'd got the wrong guy. Wayne was viciously beaten by the gang, but the beating had its effect on Russell anyway and made him realise that he really wasn't welcome.

But no sooner had the Gottliebs got rid of Russell, than another heartache came knocking at their door.

Stephen was trapped inside The Waterhole when it exploded at the beginning of May 1994. The injuries he sustained left him wheelchair bound, putting a great strain on their marriage.

Stephen thought that he was a liability to Phoebe now, and decided she would have a better chance of happiness if he wasn't around – after all, she had Hope to take care of so she didn't need him as well.

Thankfully the couple came to their senses before they got round to divorce proceedings, and as they learnt to accept Stephen's condition together, he started to get slightly better.

However, when he came face to face with his long lost brother Mark at a party, the shock sent his condition into a relapse. The neighbours thought Stephen would be thrilled to be reunited with his brother, but it was clear that Mark was not someone Stephen wanted in Erinsborough.

However, he had no choice. Mark had already landed himself the chef's job at Lassiter's (he'd only got the job by putting on a phoney French accent and pretending his name was Marcel!) and it was clear Mark intended to stay – especially as both Gaby and Annalise were happy to fight over him!

The reason the brothers fell out went back to when Stephen had been engaged to Libby. Mark,

Stephen and Libby had been at a party, where Mark spiked Stephen's drink so that he was incapable of driving home. Libby had to drive home by herself.

Tragically, the car crashed and Libby was killed. Ever since, Stephen had been unable to forgive his big brother for what he saw as causing Libby's death.

Mark on the other hand was determined to make his peace with Stephen, especially after he acquired such a soft spot for Hope and he became determined to play a part in his niece's life.

But it was obvious that Mark's presence was upsetting Phoebe and Stephen, and during one hospital visit Wayne had to punch Mark to keep him away. This led Mark to suggest that Wayne and Phoebe were having an affair, but the truth was Phoebe was very devoted to her husband.

In June 1994, things started looking up for Stephen. Not only did he come to an understanding with Mark (the breakthrough came when they were chatting idly about their days on the commune with their parents when Mark was called Cosmic, and the brothers realised that they really did have a lot in common) but on a day out in the park, Stephen managed to catch a frisbee with his bad hand. At last, it looked as if Phoebe's faith in him was going to pay off, and Stephen knew that if he could catch a frisbee, one day he would be able to walk again too.

And that day wasn't all that far off. During Helen's birthday party in the 2000th episode, Stephen gingerly took his first steps to a new future.

THE MANGELS

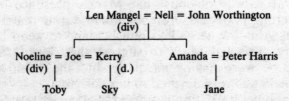

Poor old Len Mangel was so henpecked by his witch of a wife Nell that he never dared show his face in Ramsay Street!

Nell often talked off camera to Len but he was never seen and he never answered back, and slowly Mrs Mangel's neighbours began to wonder if Len was just a figment of her imagination!

The residents of Ramsay Street were always quick to speculate about Mrs Mangel's life, simply because she took so much pleasure in gossiping about everyone else's. She was interfering, self-righteous and sometimes downright malicious. If anything ever happened in Ramsay Street, the curtains at Number 32 could be guaranteed to be twitching!

One day, Mrs Mangel discovered that Len had done a runner and was cowering off camera no more. She seemed distraught that she had been deserted (being married carried certain cachet for

Nell) but it wasn't long before she'd shipped in someone else to bully. The victim was Jane Harris, her granddaughter.

Jane's mum Amanda was going overseas on business for a long time, and as she had just split from Jane's dad Peter, it was thought the best place for Jane was at her gran's. What they didn't predict was that Jane would fall head over heels for her new neighbour, Mike Young.

However, Jane thought that Mike would never notice her. After all, he never saw her in anything but her school uniform and geeky glasses, and he thought of her as simply Plain Jane Superbrain.

But with a little help from Daphne and Helen, Jane was transformed from ugly duckling to stunning swan for a school dance – and Mike was hooked!

Naturally, Mrs Mangel was suitably disapproving of the blossoming romance, and she did her level best to keep Jane from seeing Mike. However, she was often far too busy sticking her nose into other people's business, so the two teenagers managed to grab enough time alone together.

Mrs Mangel and Mike fought over another Ramsay Street resident – Bouncer, the dog. Bouncer had been Mike's pet since he was a puppy, but the mutt found himself strangely drawn to Number 32 and its owner. Mrs Mangel resented the dog at first and berated Mike for letting his dog terrorise the neighbourhood!

Slowly though, she came to see Bouncer as her only true friend in Ramsay Street, and when she knew no one was looking, Mrs M let down her guard and fed him!

Mike was a little bit peeved that Bouncer should prefer the mealy-mouthed woman to him, but agreed to let Bouncer decide where he wanted to live. So Mike let his dog off the lead in the middle of Ramsay Street to see which owner he preferred, and the kindly dog decided to be a companion for the decidedly lonely Nell Mangel.

Jane and Mike often found themselves playing second fiddle to Scott and Charlene, but occasionally they found themselves in the limelight. Like the time when Jane was 'discovered' while working as Paul's secretary and became the first Lassiter's Girl, the model around whom an important advertising campaign was built. Mike got in on the act too, as he was the photographer.

Nell, naturally, was horrified. How could her own flesh and blood take part in anything so tasteless? She also knew that a career in modelling would take Jane a step further away from the university place the Mangel family expected of her.

It soon became clear that university was no longer part of Jane's ambition as her career with the Daniels Corporation took off. Clients were impressed with her looks and her ability and it was obvious that Jane Harris would go far without any more education.

Nevertheless, when Scott Robinson needed help revising for his HSC retakes, he turned to Jane for tutoring.

At the time, Scott and Charlene's marriage was going through a rocky patch, so when Scott and Jane realised the chemistry between them had nothing to do with Scott's homework it wasn't long before they found themselves kissing.

What they didn't know was that their clinch was being witnessed by Charlene's brother Henry, and soon Jane was being painted as a bitter seductress trying to break up her best mate's marriage. Scott defended her saying that it was he who had kissed her, but Charlene was having none of it and threw Scott out and sent Jane to Coventry.

Jane decided to take herself out of the picture for a while to let the dust settle, and went abroad for a conference. When she returned, Scott was still living at his dad's and Jane realised it was up to her to get the newlyweds back together. Wearing a sharp new business suit that was more Beverly Hills than Erinsborough, Jane stormed round to Number 24 and told Charlene to buck up: if she didn't want Scott then she would have him!

Of course it was just a bluff, Jane had no interest in Scott any more, but the showdown had served its purpose. Charlene had realised that if she didn't swallow her pride then she would lose Scott forever, and so she went next door for a tearful reunion with her husband.

Charlene still refused to talk to Jane, however, and so Jane realised that she was probably better off out of Ramsay Street. She made plans to work overseas again, and her old friend Mike (they were no longer lovers, but still very close friends) arranged to take her to the airport on his motorbike. Scott and a reluctant Charlene followed in their car.

Out of nowhere came a car that was out of control – and heading straight for Mike and Jane. Mike swerved to miss the car and his bike fell to the side of the road. Jane had been thrown from the bike and it looked like she had been seriously injured.

Charlene's first instinct was to comfort Jane and in the panic of the moment confessed that Jane was still her best friend.

This confession meant Jane felt safe to return

home, where her gran was still gossiping like a trooper. By now, Mrs Mangel and Madge Ramsay had become sworn enemies, doing battle as often as they could. Whether it was over baking cakes for the church bazaar, or trying to prove that each was holier than the other.

Mrs M thought she'd really scored a few points off Madge when Helen offered to paint her portrait. Her lipsticked smile soon disintegrated when she saw the painting which was more Picasso than she would have liked! Nevertheless, pride made her display the portrait in her hall above the phone.

The Mangel house was sent into disarray when Amanda returned home from Hong Kong, and she was not pleased to see that her little girl had grown up. In an attempt to make her mother happy, Jane took off her make-up and put her hair back into bunches. Amanda brought out the worst in her mother too, and suddenly the viewers had great sympathy for Mrs Mangel – Amanda was even worse than she was!

Jane and her gran joined forces in their anger at Amanda's upsetting of the status quo, and consequently her visit brought them closer together. Sighs of relief were heard when Amanda announced that she and Peter were going to try for a reconciliation – away from Erinsborough.

Romance was on the cards for both Jane and Nell in 1990. Jane had always spent a lot of time at the Clarkes' house at Number 28 because of her relationship with Mike. But even after Mike left Erinsborough for a teacher training course, Jane stil spent much of her free time playing with little Jamie, and consequently she became very close to Des.

She had always been mature for her age, so

perhaps it wasn't so surprising that Jane developed a crush on Des. However, widower Des was still so in love with Daphne that he failed to notice how Jane felt.

Jane then had an even older man, a wealthy American client of Lassiter's called Mark. Things between them quickly became serious and he proposed. Jane accepted, but Mike's return to Ramsay Street made her realise that she didn't really love Mark, and for a brief time, Jane and Mike became close again.

But it was Des that Jane was still carrying a torch for, and in the end, Jane was forced to state her feelings and open herself up to rejection, but after Des overcame his shock he realised that he cared for Jane too, and pretty soon they got engaged.

Mrs Mangel, on the other hand, was falling for someone her own age, an English gentleman called John Worthington. Although her neighbours hated her, they all hoped that the romance would lead to marriage as it was the only way short of murder they could envisage getting rid of her! John finally proposed and they were married before the end of the year.

Mrs Mangel left Ramsay Street for a new life in England because the actress who played her, Vivean Gray, had become tired of the abuse she received in the street from people who couldn't tell her apart from her character. She'd had bricks thrown through her windows (as had the residents of the Mangels' house in Pin Oak Court) and been taunted wherever she went. Although in some strange way the abuse was a compliment as it meant she did her job very well, it was hard to see the harassment as praise, and so Vivean – and Mrs M – left Erinsborough.

But not before Nell's oikish son, Joe, arrived from

Darwin for the wedding. Joe was everything that his sister wasn't. Where Amanda had been over-achieving and shrewish, Joe was laid back and gentle.

He did however share one trait with his sister – a marriage in trouble. In fact the rows with his wife Noeline (with whom he had a son, Toby) were a major reason for his visit to see his mum. And when it was obvious that her house was going to have a spare room after the wedding, Joe decided to stay put.

For a couple of months, elegant Jane tried to put up with Joe's beer cans and TAB receipts littering the place, but it was clear that living with her yobbish uncle wasn't going to be easy. So when the offer of work in England came up, Jane decided to make the break both from Ramsay Street and Des.

The scriptwriters were never going to allow Joe to have Number 32 to himself, and so Noeline arrived on his doorstep with a present – their nine-year-old son Toby!

The viewers were surprised to see Joe become a superdad. He treated Toby (or Tobes, as he called him) like an adult and in turn Toby behaved like one.

Joe took on the traditional Erinsborough profession of self-employed gardener and wore the same set of khaki dungarees that the wardrobe department had given Shane, Clive, and Henry before him!

When he met stuffy Harold Bishop's daughter Kerry it was love at first sight. Kerry was also a single parent (to baby Sky) but that was where the similarities with Joe ended. Kerry cared about the environment, hardly drank and considered the consequences of her actions before blustering into a hasty decision. But somehow they made the perfect couple and it wasn't long before they exchanged marriage vows.

Kerry – who kept her maiden name, although she did allow people to call her *Mrs* Bishop – was very popular with the local teenagers, especially Melissa Jarrett who shared her views on the environment. It was Melissa who told Kerry about the tests on mice in the science labs at school, and together the two women plotted to set the mice free.

The school principal and new neighbour, Dorothy Burke, accused Melissa of committing the crime, so Kerry was forced to confess that she had done the deed. Mrs Burke very nearly called the police, but she – like everyone else – was impressed by the depth of Kerry's convictions, and so she let the matter rest.

Toby loved his new stepmum, and although it was an unusual set-up, the Mangel clan were the closest family in Ramsay Street. To show how he felt about Kerry, Toby asked if she would mind if he called her 'mum' now that Noeline had died. Kerry replied that nothing would make her happier, especially as she was now pregnant with Joe's child.

Ironically, it was to be Kerry's commitment to preserve the planet for future generations that led to her own untimely death. She was so determined to stop a game shoot by poachers that Joe only agreed to let her go if he went with her to protect her. But he couldn't protect her from a stray bullet.

Kerry was thrown to the ground by the force of the shot. Joe ran to his wife through the waist-high reeds and knee-deep mud, but it was too late. Just as he reached Kerry, she died in his arms.

Joe was devastated, as was Kerry's dad Harold. Still, at least they had Sky, and as long as Kerry's little girl was around then Kerry would always be with them.

But soon after Kerry's death, Sky's natural father Eric Jensen announced he would fight for custody of the child. Toby and Joe were distraught – she was part of their family now.

But Eric was insistent: he had reformed from his hippy days of Sky's conception and was now a respectable businessman, with a respectable suit and a wife to match.

Joe fought for custody in the courts, but the judge felt the little girl should be with her natural father. Toby and Joe pined for Sky, so when Ian announced that he couldn't cope with being a father the Mangels welcomed her back with open arms. And Harold was thrilled to have his granddaughter back in Ramsay Street too.

Joe's trusty lodger Melanie Pearson helped Joe look after the kids who began to treat her like a mum. It slowly dawned on Joe that he might have fallen in love with Melanie, who had previously dated Henry Ramsay.

Melanie was one of Ramsay Street's most delightful residents. With her infectious seal-like laugh she endeared herself to all the neighbours (except maybe Paul who was her boss and found her just a little too scatty).

But just as Joe plucked up the courage to ask Melanie out on a date, she started seeing a Lassiter's client called Simon Hunter. Joe thought he'd lost her for sure when she announced that she and Simon were getting engaged.

Joe looked for love on a *Blind Date*-style TV show called *Dream Date*. On the night he was due to take part, one of the other contestants fell through and typically Melanie ended joking her way on to the set to become one of the mystery contestants. And as fate would have it, Joe picked Mel to be his date and gladly shared his prize with her – a romantic holiday for two!

On the first night of their trip, Joe called Mel from his hotel room and asked to meet her. Their stilted, stuttering conversation revealed to each other how they really felt, and they rushed out into the hotel hallway and fell into each other's arms and kissed.

Viewers all round the world cheered for them and the sighs of 'ahh' were deafening. There was just one problem – telling Simon. Naturally he wasn't very happy, but there was nothing he could do about it – Joe and Melanie had found each other and they weren't giving up.

They married in October 1992, and when they left for their honeymoon, they took with them the best wishes of everybody in Erinsborough. Even Harold was thrilled to see that Joe had found someone after Kerry.

Joe and Melanie took little Sky with them on their tour of Europe (they later settled in England near Joe's mum when she was taken ill) but they carelessly left behind Toby and Bouncer!

The young lad was taken in by Dorothy Burke next door, who had also 'acquired' another orphaned school kid, Phoebe Bright.

Dorothy got an unexpected second chance at love in 1993 when she met education inspector Tom Merrick. And when Tom and Dorothy started a new life together in the country, they took Toby with them. Bouncer went to Anson's Corner where he had fathered a litter of puppies!

THE MARTIN FAMILY

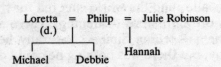

THE MARTIN FAMILY TREE

Loretta = Philip = Julie Robinson
(d.)

Michael   Debbie   Hannah

For someone so annoying, Julie Robinson never had any problems attracting the men! At one point she was going out with neighbour Des Clarke, and shortly after they broke up she fell for her new boss at the Pacific Bank, Philip Martin.

There was just one snag – Philip was married with two kids. However, his marriage was a sham. His wife Loretta was a drunk who took more care of the bar staff at the local pub than she did of her kids, Michael and Debbie.

Even so, Philip would not cheat on his wife. But the situation changed dramatically when Loretta and Philip were involved in a car accident. Loretta had been drunk at the wheel and died instantly, Philip on the other hand was left paralysed and in a wheelchair.

The Robinsons assumed that Julie would lose interest in Philip now that he could no longer walk or provide her with the good things in life, but she surprised them all when she announced that she

72

was giving up her work to look after Philip and his kids.

And so she left Ramsay Street in 1987 and very little was heard from her until 1993 when she returned with her family to Erinsborough for Todd Landers' funeral.

In her years away from the screen Julie married and had a daughter of her own, Hannah, and yet this had never been mentioned! Very, very rarely Jim might be heard having a conversation with her on the phone, and occasionally the scriptwriters would remember that Julie ought to send a telegram to important Robinson events, but basically Julie had been forgotten!

Her return was slightly forced as Julie and Todd had never actually met, and yet this was the device used to lure her back to town!

On her return it was immediately apparent that she hadn't changed (except her looks of course – in true *Neighbours* style Julie was now played by a different actress, Julie Mullins, who replaced the original actress, Vikki Blanche). Julie was still as nosey, interfering, opinionated, annoying and insensitive as she always was. And although Jim and Helen welcomed her back with open arms, they knew she meant trouble. Julie and Philip had another reason for their homecoming as well as Todd's funeral – they were in dire financial straits and needed help. They moved into Number 26 with Jim and Helen while they tried to get back on their feet. (Philip, miraculously, was literally back on his feet as the scriptwriters had forgotten his paralysis in the intervening years!)

Philip was a kind and proud man who put up with his wife's annoying little ways as he was always grateful for the way Julie had given up her life for him and his kids. But when Julie got a job with her brother Paul at Lassiter's, Philip felt that he should do more to provide for his family.

When he took the job of caretaker at Erinsborough High, his daughter Debbie was mortified. Being the new kid in school was embarrassing enough without having the added nightmare of having your dad as the lowly janitor. (Debbie would be further embarrassed a year later when Julie decided to return to school.)

In the end it was Debbie's uncle Paul who saved her from her blushes when he installed Philip as the new boss at Lassiter's when Benito Alessi failed to make the grade. But just as it seemed the Martins were sorting themselves out, Philip's son from his first marriage turned up like a bad penny.

Michael Martin was bad through and through. He got his kicks out of hurting people and causing grief, and he derived pure pleasure in making his stepmother miserable.

Although Philip knew that Michael was hard to have around for Julie, he was not ready to write off his only son. Hannah and Debbie were caught in the middle of the family feud, but eventually Julie managed to prove to a reluctant Debbie that Michael had always had it in for her.

Michael's hate was deep seated: it turned out that he blamed Julie for his mother's death believing that Philip's friendship with Julie had been what had driven Loretta to drink.

But all the explanations in the world cut no ice with the vindictive teenager who decided the only way to get Julie out of his life was to kill her.

First of all he managed to convince the rest of the

family and Julie herself that she was losing her marbles. He'd make phonecalls from round the corner on a mobile phone and then turn up on the doorstep seconds later, convincing Julie that she had imagined the phone call.

Julie's behaviour became even more odd when Michael made her doubt her own sanity, and few of the neighbours were willing to support her (by now she had infuriated everyone in the street). So when Julie was persuaded to take some pills to calm her down and ease her mind, everyone was too relieved at the thought of slowing down her motor mouth to warn her against taking the medication.

Michael's plan was starting to take shape. He intended to slip extra pills into Julie's drink and food to make her drowsy. If she took enough, he was sure he would be able to kill her without anyone suspecting foul play. He first tried to execute his plan at Phoebe and Stephen's wedding, where everyone thought Julie was extremely drunk and rude.

He may not have managed to kill her that time, but Michael had made her so obnoxious that Philip came one step closer to asking for a divorce. Michael made several more attempts on his stepmother's life and no one suspected a thing. Even when Rick and Debbie found Julie virtually comatose in the spa in the garden with Michael standing by and doing nothing, he still managed to avoid suspicion.

But Julie herself had begun to notice a pattern in her drugged episodes, and slowly she twigged that it had something to do with Michael. It was only when she looked at the video of the Gottliebs' wedding that she finally found her proof.

In the background at the party she spied Michael

placing a drug into her champagne. It was the proof she needed to convince Debbie and Philip that Michael had to leave.

Unlike her brother, Debbie got on extremely well with Julie – indeed the two women often seemed more like sisters – and she also enjoyed life in Ramsay Street a whole lot more than Michael, because she had found love!

Cute Rick Alessi from Number 22 quickly became her paramour, but their passion for pranks – as well as each other – frequently got them into trouble with their parents and principal Dorothy Burke.

But all the attempts to keep the canoodling teenagers apart failed, and in the end the Alessis and the Martins had to concede that it was less trouble letting them see each other than it was trying to come between them.

However, when Rick and Debbie won a trip to London to see Michael Jackson in concert they both knew there was no way their parents would let them go. So with the help of Rick's elder brother Marco and Debbie's gran Helen, they devised a plan to sneak them to London without their 'olds' knowing.

It worked! But just when it looked like they'd got away with it, a TV show they had appeared on in London was shown in Australia and their ruse was rumbled! On their return they were both grounded, but as always it proved fruitless to separate them and soon they were up to their old tricks.

The truth was Philip was far more worried about Michael than he was about Debbie's love life. He hadn't heard from his son in months and he was starting to fear the worst. In an attempt to find out where Michael was, Philip hired a detective agency to track him down. But knowing how Julie felt about Michael, Philip kept the sleuthing secret from his wife.

But when Gaby Willis, who was Philip's assistant at Lassiter's, noticed that some of her boss's money was going to a mysterious agency she thought that Philip was hiring escorts. Before she jumped to any conclusions, Gaby decided to follow Philip and see if he saw anyone mysterious.

When she traced him to the seedy side of town she thought her suspicions were confirmed. Julie too began to doubt her husband's fidelity when he bought Gaby flowers. Philip tried to explain that he was just thanking his employee for her good work, but Julie went as far as to accuse him of having an affair.

This was the final straw for Philip and he asked Julie for a divorce.

They were soon reconciled, but it was abundantly clear that their marriage had severe difficulties. In an effort to make Julie happy, Philip decided to work out and shape up after a throw-away comment from Julie that he was getting a bit portly.

When Julie noticed that Philip was at work in different clothes to those he was wearing in the morning, she began to have doubts about Philip's faithfulness again. And when she noticed that he was often coming home late she again feared the worst and confronted him.

Philip was angry that she had doubted him again, but set her straight by announcing that he had been seeing a personal trainer called Arnie. Julie apologised for her foolishness, but the cracks in their marriage were now plain to see.

Still there was some good news for Philip when Rick spotted Michael selling watches on the beach during a trip to Sydney. Debbie and Philip paid the wayward Michael a visit where they had an emotional reunion and called a truce.

Philip tried to persuade Michael to return to Erinsborough, but when his son explained he preferred life on the road, Philip was forced to leave Michael to do his own thing – but not before Philip had thrust a fistful of dollars on Michael.

They returned to Ramsay Street where Julie was more than pleased to realise Michael was not with them. However, tragedy was just round the corner for Julie as her father Jim was about to suffer a fatal heart attack. While she was still grieving for her father, she was further upset by the arrival of her stepson on the front porch. She told him calmly that she didn't want him in the house and that she didn't appreciate him turning up unexpectedly. She closed the door in his face and Michael stayed waiting for his dad to come home.

But before Philip got back from the office, Michael collapsed and was unconscious when his dad came home. Philip rushed his son to hospital and told Julie that he could never forgive her for shutting the door in his face. Julie explained that she had no idea he was ill, but Philip was having none of it.

However, before she could get too involved in her matrimonial discord, Julie would have to face one of the toughest tests of her life.

Following Jim's death, Helen read through some of the love letters Jim and her daughter Anne had written to each other when they were first married. In one of the letters Helen uncovered some disturbing news – Julie was not Jim's daughter.

Helen wrestled with her conscience, but finally told her granddaughter the disturbing truth. Julie could not rest until she found her natural father and set about unearthing her real roots.

She discovered her father's name was Roger Bannon and she tracked him down to Queensland. Giving few reasons she left Hannah and Philip, to seek some answers about her past. When she finally came face to face with Roger Bannon she was in for a shock – he was only a couple of years older than her and obviously wasn't her father. He was actually her half-brother, Roger Bannon Jnr.

Julie did not reveal her identity to her half-brother, and was disgusted when he made a play for her and groped her. She was so upset by the incident that she decided to look elsewhere for clues about her father.

She got the answers from Roger Bannon Snr's widow (he had passed away a few years previously) who told Julie the most awful piece of news she had ever heard.

Anne had not been having an affair with Roger – he had raped her. Julie was at once disgusted and distraught to realise she was the product of a rape, and returned to Erinsborough deeply unsettled and unsure.

The first thing she did on arrival was tell Philip that she wanted a divorce and expected custody of Hannah. Philip understood her desire for a divorce was because she felt the marriage was over, but the truth was that Julie felt she was no longer desirable or worthy since she'd learnt about her conception. And she was so disgusted by the truth that she didn't tell a soul – not even Helen.

Philip moved into the accommodation at Lassiter's where Gaby was taking on more and more of his workload in an obvious play for his job.

Julie stayed on in Ramsay Street with Hannah and Debbie who was becoming increasing worried about her little sister who had started bed-wetting regularly. Debbie tried to explain to her stepmum that constant rows with Philip were taking their toll on Hannah.

Hannah's well-being had virtually been ignored. Because she was a bright child who rarely caused them bother, Julie and Philip had got used to assuming she was always all right. When she wanted a party – they gave her one; when she wanted to keep Holly the puppy – they let her.

But the constant slanging matches had upset the little girl deeply, and Julie soon realised that she would have to do better by her daughter. She decided to make use of the 50% stake in the car yard that Jim had left her in his will and earn enough to support her little girl.

Julie proved to be an unusually successful saleswoman, especially with female customers, and so she and Lou Carpenter made a good team.

However, her financial independence brought divorce another step closer. Philip maintained daily contact with his daughters as well as making regular visits to Michael who was now in Borstal. Michael made no attempt to hide his glee when Philip told him about the impending divorce.

Life on the inside wasn't easy for Michael who was being bullied. When a rival, Darren Starke, threatened to 'get' Debbie when he was released, Michael knew he had to break out of jail to protect his sister. With the help of Rick, who had now split with Debbie after her dalliance with Harvey, the Lassiter's chef, Michael scaled the perimeter fence and broke free. He then had to disguise himself by wearing women's clothing!

The two lads managed to keep Debbie from serious harm when they interrupted a petrol station raid Darren had lured Debbie into. In a struggle with a gun, Michael took a bullet in the chest and was rushed to casualty.

Relations between Julie and Philip were still strained while Michael recovered in hospital, but they made a special effort for Helen's birthday (featured in the 2000th episode).

On the day of the party, Paul Robinson, who had flown in from Hawaii, had to tell Philip that he was definitely giving the top Lassiter's job to Gaby Willis, but Phil had something much more important on his mind – a reunion with his wife.

Julie told Philip about the disturbing news she'd learnt in Queensland, and Philip reassured Julie that it didn't matter to him that she was the result of a rape. Reassured by her husband's love, Julie vowed to bury her past and look forward to her future – with Philip.

THE RAMSAYS

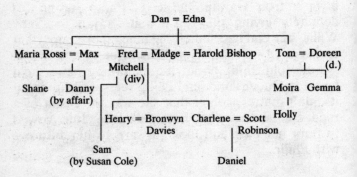

The Ramsays are the royal family of *Neighbours* and their claim on Erinsborough goes back generations. The pride they have in 'their' street has led them to be brash and arrogant. It's easy to spot a Ramsay – they'll be the loudest people in the room and may well be talking themselves into a fight!

When *Neighbours* first started in 1985, the occupiers of Number 24 were Max Ramsay and his European wife Maria, and their two sons, Shane and Danny.

Although they were usually good friends with the Robinsons next door, there was a lot of tension between the two families when the show began because Jim Robinson was dating Maria's sister, Anna Rossi.

In the end, Anna left Jim and Erinsborough and the tension died down. On the surface the Ramsays now seemed a happy, strong family. Max was hardworking, Maria was beautiful, Shane was athletic and Danny was academic. But within weeks, the cracks started to show.

Maria thought her macho husband took her for granted, Shane resented his dad for pushing him to train for the Olympic diving team, and Danny and Max were constantly at each other's throats.

Danny had been having unexplained nightmares for months (in fact he spoke the first words ever said in *Neighbours* when he tussled in his sleep crying out 'No, no, Shane, no, no') and it was clear he was a troubled teenager.

So when Maria revealed that Danny was not Max's son but the product of an affair, Max resented the boy even more and stormed out to live in a rented bedsit.

Another blow came when a car crash put paid to Shane's Olympic diving hopes – it was also a blow to female viewers who would no longer see handsome actor Peter O'Brien in his Speedos every episode! – and when Maria started dating an insurance salesman called Richard Morris, it seemed the Ramsay Street marriage was well and truly over.

But there was also trouble off-camera for the Ramsays and it wasn't long before Maria, actress Dasha Blahova, was packed off to Brisbane; David Clencie who played Danny was allegedly asked to leave for being difficult; and Francis Bell who played the bullish Max made the fatal mistake of asking for more money. It wasn't long before the scriptwriters engineered a hasty reconciliation with Maria, and Max too headed north.

That left just Shane, who was enjoying an on-screen flirtation with sensible stripper Daphne Lawrence, when in real life Peter O'Brien was dating the actress who played her, Elaine Smith.

The producers soon installed some new Ramsays in Number 24. First there was Madge Mitchell for whom conversation was less of an art, more of a way of life!

Madge's appearance in Ramsay Street was shortly followed by the arrival of her younger brother Tom, a carbon copy of his older brother Max, who took over not just the house but also the plumbing business, and evidently also his wardrobe of overalls and dungarees. Tom was a widower who had recently lost his wife Doreen with whom he'd had a happy marriage and two daughters, Moira and Gemma.

Where her brothers were blustering fools, Madge was interfering and pompous. She was also a snob and it was to her great shame that her husband Fred had run off with his secretary, her son Henry was in jail and her daughter Charlene had gone off the rails.

Madge pretended that she didn't like to gossip – such tittle-tattle was beneath her – but in actual fact she thrived on being nosey and keeping her finger in everybody else's pies. It was obvious that she and Nell Mangel were destined to be the best of enemies!

It wasn't long before Shane had had enough of the bickering in the house that had been his home longer than anyone else and he moved into the caravan at the Lassiter's lake. This made way for the arrival of Charlene, who had hitched her way from Coffs

Harbour to Erinsborough, where she was caught breaking into her mother's house by neighbour Scott Robinson.

It was an unlikely start to *Neighbours*' hottest ever romance, but that's how TV's most celebrated teen lovers met.

Charlene brought with her some tales Madge hoped the neighbours would never know, and some outfits she hoped they'd never see! It turned out that Charlene had developed a taste for alcohol and loud clothes at an early age, and the guys had developed a taste for her! It was revealed that teenage Charlene had already had an abortion and been on the Pill – it was clear this girl was going to be trouble. No wonder Jim didn't want Scott seeing her. (Madge was equally disapproving of their love affair as she worried Charlene might get pregnant again!)

But this was *Neighbours*, the soap that got whites whiter than white, and no such impropriety was going to be shown on screen.

Madge would never have admitted it, but her daughter was a chip off the old block – cunning, mouthy and not very good at showing her emotion. ('She'd rather die than be caught crying,' commented actress Kylie Minogue.)

Madge so wanted to be proud of her kids, if only to score points off Mrs Mangel, but unfortunately she felt they had both let her down and wasn't best pleased when Lennie (as Charlene liked to be known) told her she intended to be a garage mechanic.

When Charlene arrived home one day in 1987 with a baby, it seemed perfectly plausible that the little boy was hers. But in fact baby Sam was her half-brother, the product of Fred's fling with his secretary Susan Cole.

Fred had run off with the money Madge had sent him to save the family business (money Madge had raised by selling her diamond ring), in another of his trademark selfish acts.

So when Charlene finally confessed that she hadn't been a gymslip mum and brought Susan round to the Ramsay house, Madge knew not to blame Susan for breaking up her marriage – Fred was just a rat.

Although Susan and Sam stayed with Madge and her family for a while, they quickly moved in with Clive Gibbons at Number 22, although it took Susan months to realise that Clive was hopelessly in love with her.

The Mitchell women proved to be too much for poor old Tom to cope with, so when he learnt that he had become a grandfather by his estranged daughter, Moira Harrigan, he decided to pay little Holly a visit and left Ramsay Street.

Just when it looked like Erinsborough was finally free of the arrogant Ramsay men, Dan Ramsay arrived to show the neighbours that they'd got off lightly till then!

It was immediately apparent where Tom and Max got their pig-headedness from – Dan was worse than both of them put together! And he was particularly annoying at that time because he and Edna, his wife of nearly fifty years, were on the brink of divorce.

It seemed he'd had enough of her nagging and she had endured as much as she could take of his eye for the ladies. The final straw for Edna had been Dan's pathetic flirtation with Rosie Jacobs from the bowling club – a woman half his age. Like her daughter, Edna was very big on what the neighbours thought, and the embarrassment of his latest fling meant she could no longer hold her head high at the club.

Madge was very upset at the thought of her parents splitting up, and together with Mr Gift of the Gab himself, Clive Gibbons, she engineered a plan to bring her mum and dad back together.

But all attempts failed and Edna decided to press ahead with the divorce. But she was in for a shock when she was told she didn't need one – it turned out that they had never legally been married!

Yes, thanks to Dan's typical incompetence, the wedding certificate had never actually been filed and Edna was distraught to learn that she had been living in sin for half a century. Dan was determined to make it up to her, and his attempts proved to Edna that he actually still loved her very much, and she was forced to concede that she felt the same way too.

And so before they returned to Brisbane they were officially married, making it legal after all those years.

However, it wasn't long before another loud and brash Ramsay man had his feet under the table at Number 24. Madge's jailbird son Henry was finally released from prison after previous false alarms in the guise of actor Craig McLachlan.

Henry – who was the spitting image of his screen sister with matching curly blond hair, too many teeth, and grubby overalls – was the holy goof of *Neighbours*. He had a devilish sense of fun, and just about everyone enjoyed his company. He was loud and he was wacky and it was hard to believe that he had ever been 'inside', but the prejudice he suffered when he applied for jobs was testament enough to his earlier bad boy ways.

In the end he decided it was easier to be self-employed, and so Henry borrowed his cousin Shane's dungarees and started mowing lawns for a living. Although Madge would have liked something more for her son, she couldn't really complain – after all, she was only the barmaid at The Waterhole, and tee total Madge had a hard time dealing with her leather skinned and leather livered customers. (She had originally been Paul's secretary, but her interfering ways meant Paul quickly found an alternative position for her!)

Henry and Charlene had a typical brother/sister relationship and either bickered or squabbled. But they joined forces when it came to setting up their mum with her childhood sweetheart, Harold Bishop.

Madge had shown Charlene her High School Dance photos and mentioned Harold's name. Charlene then turned amateur sleuth and tracked Harold down only to find that he was, by coincidence, about to make a trip to Erinsborough!

Harold was a real stuffed shirt and he made Madge look like a loose woman! He was a church-going, vegetarian prude, but his blustering ways had a certain charm and Madge was hooked. They even went out and bought matching shell suits!

Harold helped Madge cope when Charlene announced that she was going to marry Scott – at just 17! The two teenagers had finally started dating after they were left alone together babysitting for little Jamie Clarke, and ever since it had been 'full on'!

Scott and Charlene were so in love that they announced they wanted to live together, and naturally their parents kicked up a fuss and refused to let them. Distraught at the thought of spending any time apart, Scott skateboarded over to Rob Lewis's garage where Charlene was doing apprentice work and proposed marriage. Unsurprisingly Charlene accepted. Convincing their parents it was a good idea was another matter, but their obvious love for each other soon brought the protesters round.

The knowledge that Charlene would soon be a Robinson set Madge and Henry thinking – at least she would no longer be tarnished by the Mitchell tag, a name Fred had turned to mud with every credit agency in Australia. So Madge and her son decided to change their names to Ramsay by deed poll.

The fairytale wedding of Scott and Charlene took place in November 1988, but within months it looked like the relationship was doomed. Scott thought Charlene was having an affair with her driving instructor; meanwhile, he was becoming closer and closer to Jane Harris as she tutored him for his HSC retakes.

When Jane confessed to Charlene that Scott had kissed her, Charlene threw her husband out of the Ramsay house and he moved back next door. Finally, Jane had a showdown with Charlene and told her that she could steal Scott any time she wanted. Charlene took note and claimed him for herself before it was too late, but they were only reunited for a short time before Charlene made her tearful departure to Brisbane where Dan and Edna had bought a house for them. Scott stayed living at Madge's for a while before joining his wife up north.

It wasn't long before the Ramsays were organising another wedding as Madge and Harold seemed destined to tie the knot. However that was only until old flame Lou Carpenter arrived on the scene.

Lou had been at school with Madge and Harold, and like Harold he still carried a torch for Madge. Lou was everything that Harold wasn't – impressive, amoral, reckless and fun. He was also a millionaire car salesman.

It was genuinely a tough choice for Madge, but she plumped for the cuddly Harold and they soon made it official and married.

Henry was also in love – with local nanny Bronwyn Davies, and when she was forced to leave her lodgings with Mrs Mangel, Bronwyn was invited to live – in sin – with Henry at Number 24.

Naturally this raised a few eyebrows with the neighbours – at least Scott and Charlene had had the decency to marry. And even though Madge too would have preferred the sleeping arrangements to be different, she did take some pride in knowing her new 'modern' values were ruffling Mrs Mangel's prudish feathers.

It wasn't long before Henry and Bronwyn wanted to make their relationship a little more 'traditional' and the two of them got engaged. However, just when Madge was getting used to the idea of seeing both her kids happily married, Henry announced that he was leaving.

Out of the blue he had been offered the chance to be a radio DJ in New Zealand, and the opportunity was so good that it was worth being separated from his beloved Bronwyn.

The lovers said a tearful farewell at the airport (the tears were for real as the actors who played Henry and Bronwyn, Craig McLachlan and Rachel Friend, had become lovers in real life and this meant Craig was leaving the show) and Bronwyn continued to live in the Ramsay house until she could find suitable veterinary work (she had since swapped looking after children for animal welfare) in New Zealand.

Harold's children also made an appearance in Erinsborough. His son, David, was a carbon copy of his father, right down to the slightest mannerisms, and punctuated speech, but David's elder sister Kerry seemed to be cut from different cloth.

She was a free spirit, a hippy, who had travelled round the world with a group of friends. Harold was in for a shock when she wrote to him and told him that he had become a grandfather – she'd had a daughter and named her Sky.

Life on the road was tough as a single mum, and soon Kerry returned for an emotional reunion with her father where Harold held his granddaughter for the first time.

Kerry stayed with her dad and stepmum for a while, but to everyone's amazement (and some amusement) she started dating fellow single parent, the oikish Joe Mangel. But it proved to be a case of opposites attract and they too made it legal, and Kerry moved across the street to Number 32.

But before Madge and Harold got used to having their house to themselves, it was announced that Tom's daughter Gemma was coming to live with them while her dad took a lucrative job in the bush.

Gemma, played by Beth Buchanan, was a bright kid with a sensible disposition and it was clear that her only real problem would be choosing between her many suitors. She picked Matt Robinson and the two enjoyed a successful romance until her ex turned up in Ramsay Street and put Matt's nose out of joint. He took things the wrong way and ran off to his home town of Adelaide, and in the process broke Gemma's heart.

But neighbourly Adam Willis was around to comfort her, and soon she felt a genuine attraction for him too, and the pair fell very deeply in love.

Gemma left Ramsay Street in 1991 to work for an animal sanctuary in Newcastle, New South Wales, and pretty soon afterwards Adam Willis got a transfer to the medical school there so that they could continue to be together.

But the Ramsay house was still bustling with activity. Sky and Toby (Joe's son by his first marriage to Noeline) constantly visited 'grandma and grandad', and Madge and Harold liked playing their new roles of pillars of the community.

Harold became the local scout leader, believing it to be his Christian duty to teach the youth of Erinsborough to tie reef knots! And Madge took up office when she beat principal Dorothy Burke to be a local councillor.

By now, Madge and Harold had bought the Lassiter's Coffee Shop and while Harold served up Vegetarian Surprise, Madge dished out the gossip! Sadly, their happy and hard won stability was about to be shattered by tragedy.

Kerry was killed in a shooting accident while she was protesting against poachers. The fact that she died fighting for a cause she believed in and that she died in her husband's arms was little solace for Harold, who began to question his faith in God after the accident.

It was a huge blow and it took Joe and Harold a long time before they could carry on with their lives. Madge tried to help her husband through the hardest times and suggested that they take a trip to put the heartache finally behind them. And anyway, they had had an unexpected win on the Premium Bonds and felt they deserved a break. They took a round the world holiday, and while they were in England bumped into Rosemary Daniels.

Madge and Harold obviously got the travelling bug, and in 1992 they set off again, this time to tour Australia in a caravan.

They rented the house to Brenda Riley, who would also man the Coffee Shop for them while they were away.

Brenda seemed nice enough, but Harold would have had a fit if he'd known that she was the little sister of Lou Carpenter, the man who had lost out to Harold almost five years previously.

After Madge and Harold had started on their tour, Lou's son Guy came to live with his aunt in Ramsay Street and help out in the Coffee Shop. But it wouldn't be long before Madge was returning to Erinsborough – alone.

Not long after they set out on their tour, Madge and Harold were walking along a rocky coastal path. While Madge stopped to talk to a local painter, Harold ventured closer to the edge. But when Madge started to look for her husband, Harold was nowhere to be seen.

It seemed he had fallen off the rocks and into the sea, although his body was never found.

Madge was understandably grief-stricken, and decided to take time out from her day-to-day existence and go to stay with Charlene and Scott in Brisbane and help her daughter through her first pregnancy.

When she felt strong enough, Madge – now the last of the Ramsays in Ramsay Street – returned to

Erinsborough one last time. But there was an unexpected surprise for her when she got home – Lou Carpenter.

Lou had been visiting his sister Brenda, and when he unexpectedly came face to face with his old flame, they were both surprised to find that some of the old passion was still there.

They fell into a kind of 'relationship of convenience', which Lou – who had now 'lost' his millions thanks to the scriptwriters' memory loss and had to settle for a suburban car yard – tried to spice up their sedentary relationship by proposing to Madge.

But when she couldn't say 'Yes', Madge knew that Lou wasn't the man for her, and that if she was being honest with herself she still hadn't got over Harold.

Although Madge and Lou remained friends, they agreed to part. And while Lou bought the house and set down his own foundations in Erinsborough, Madge was packing to leave.

And in true Ramsay tradition, she followed the rest of her brood to Brisbane in 1993 where she is now a proud granny to Scott and Charlene's son Daniel, and a regular letter writer to Helen Daniels who still lives in 'her' street.

THE ROBINSONS

When *Neighbours* first started, the Robinsons were an uncomplicated brood. Jim lived at Number 26 with his four bright and relatively trouble-free kids, and although his wife Anne had died, the children and the house were cared for by Jim's mother-in-law, Helen Daniels.

Jim was *Neighbours'* Mr Nice Guy. He was good to his kids, kind to his neighbours and reasonable in all circumstances. He supported his family comfortably as the partner in an engineering firm, but found he had even more time for his kids after he invented a car jack that was patented meaning he could virtually give up work.

Helen was created by Reg Watson to explode the myth that all mothers-in-law are interfering battle-axes. Not only was Helen wanted around the house, she was needed.

She listened attentively to the problems of all the Robinsons (and indeed all the neighbours) while baking the best cakes in Erinsborough and running her own chauffeuring business, Home James. She also found time to paint in her spare time.

Jim's eldest son Paul started off as quietly academic and seemed destined to follow his dad into the family business. It therefore came as a big surprise when Paul announced that he was quitting

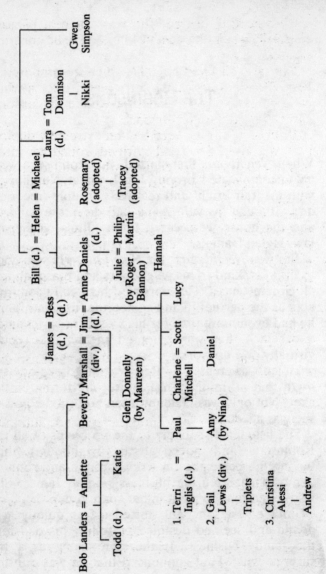

THE ROBINSON FAMILY TREE

his engineering degree. Jim was not best pleased, especially when Paul said he intended to be an airline steward!

Paul also shocked his folks when he proposed to Max Ramsay's assistant, Terri Inglis, after a whirlwind romance. But the marriage, like his airborne career, was to be short-lived.

It turned out that Terri had an extremely dubious past, and one of her ex-boyfriends roped her into a highly elaborate murder plot, which ended up with Terri killing her ex and framing Daphne Lawrence for the crime.

But when Terri overreacted to the bang of a balloon bursting, Paul began to suspect that Terri might have been the one who pulled the trigger. As he phoned to shop his wife to the police, she used the gun a second time and shot him in the shoulder.

Terri was convicted for her crimes and later committed suicide in jail, but justice was no comfort for Paul who had become calculating and bitter after the experience. And it was these qualities that led his aunt Rosemary (Helen's adopted daughter) to give him the tough and ruthless job of heading the Daniels Corporation in Australia.

Paul's younger sister Julie was equally prickly to be around but for very different reasons. Julie was an infuriating gossip who couldn't keep her nose out of other people's business. She had once dated her neighbour Des Clarke, who she also worked with at the Pacific Bank where she was a teller.

Julie was not very popular as her interfering ways got up everybody's noses. So when she left Erinsborough in 1987 to care for widowed (and paralysed) bank manager Philip Martin and his two kids, the neighbourhood heaved a collective sigh of relief.

Jim's other son, Scott, was the first character in *Neighbours* to undergo a severe sea change in appearance. He was originally played by a dark haired actor called Darius Perkins, but after Channel Ten picked up the show and Perkins had stepped out of line once too often, Scott got lost in the bush and was discovered a few weeks later looking very healthy, lovely and blond. Scott was now portrayed by Jason Donovan, who turned Scott into every girl's dream date.

As well as being impossibly cute, Scott was witty and charming. He looked out for his little sister Lucy, and looked up to and respected his dad. He was reasonably bright and stood every chance of realising his ambition of becoming a journalist.

Lucy, the youngest of the Robinson clan, was eight years younger than Scott and had quite a different childhood to her siblings. Anne, her mother, died giving birth to her and so the most formative influence in her life was her gran, Helen.

Paul and Julie doted on their little sister and consequently Lucy seemed spoilt at times, although Scott was always on hand for a bit of sibling bickering. Like her elder brother, Lucy also miraculously changed her appearance. When she was packed off to boarding school at 11 she was played by Kylie Flinker, but when she came home for her vacation she looked a lot older and was played by Sasha Close!

In the nine years that *Neighbours* has been going, each member of this remarkable family has endured enough trauma to put most people into an early grave! It seems these Robinson folk have invincibility running through their veins.

Helen has had more heartbreak than all of them

put together. The first major blow was when her beloved husband Bill died in the early seventies. And she was to mourn again a few years later when her daughter Anne died in childbirth. As Helen desperately loved her grandchildren, and as baby Lucy needed someone to care for her, she offered to move in with her son-in-law Jim and be a surrogate mother to her grandchildren.

Helen's heart of gold also extends to taking care of lost souls she's not related to, and throughout the years she has been the confidante of many of the neighbours.

She is the most glamorous granny on TV, and as well as being an ace housekeeper, she also proved sprightly in the business world when – as well as running Home James – she also helped Paul manage Lassiter's and the Daniels Corporation in the early days.

In her spare time – and there's not a lot of it – Helen paints and she has even had a couple of exhibitions. At her first public exhibition she met a man called Douglas Blake (who was actually played by Anne Haddy's real life husband James Condon) and she fell in love with him.

He persuaded her that they should buy property together, but she discovered just too late that Douglas was a con-man who robbed her of her life savings.

Helen's heart was sorely broken, and she therefore took much joy in finding her revenge several months later when he tried the same trick on another woman, unaware that it was Helen's friend, Madge!

Over the years, Helen has taken it upon herself to care for several waifs and strays, and at various times has invited homeless souls to live with her. They include struggling artist Nick Page, Josh Anderson and even the youth that mugged her, Greg Bartlett.

Naturally, Helen is universally trusted (she never gossips like Madge or Mrs Mangel) and respected, so when she suffered a serious stroke in 1988 and subsequently went into a coma, the whole street rallied round and took it in turns to sit with her in hospital. Mercifully, everybody's favourite neighbour pulled through with no long-term damage.

When Helen met and fell in love with Michael Daniels – her late husband's cousin – everyone in Ramsay Street was delighted for her. He seemed to be perfect – charming, sensitive and funny. But Michael Daniels was hiding a heartbreaking secret – he was already married.

This shocking fact was uncovered while Helen was on her honeymoon, but the rest of the Robinsons thought it best to wait until she returned home before telling her. She was devastated that yet again a man she loved had tried to con her. This time it was Helen who needed the advice and consoling.

Jim's love life has been equally unsuccessful. When *Neighbours* began, he was dating Maria Ramsay's sister Anna, who eventually left him because she didn't want to cause a feud between the Ramsays and the Robinsons.

His next screen love was two years later (actor Alan Dale once commented that Jim was too celibate to be believable!) when he fell for Zoe Davis – a woman twenty years his junior!

Zoe was one of life's genuine eccentrics. She was madcap and forgetful, but these characteristics, which infuriated her boss Paul, enticed his father.

The affair got unexpectedly serious when Zoe fell pregnant. Gentleman Jim offered to do the decent thing and marry her, but Zoe turned him down. They stayed together anyway and made tentative plans for the future, but they were sadly and dramatically robbed of that future when Zoe suffered an ectopic pregnancy and miscarried.

Jim's next romance was with British traveller Ruth Wilson. They met on a plane on his way back from America and got on like a house on fire. Jim mentioned that his son ran a hotel, and when the plane touched down Ruth checked into Lassiter's.

But when she couldn't pay her bill, Paul seized her luggage until it was settled. Jim stepped into the breach and not only paid her bill but asked her to stay with him until her financial problems in England were sorted out. Sadly it transpired that Ruth was just another in a long line of Ramsay Street swindlers trying to squeeze as much money out of Jim as possible.

It was to be third time lucky for Jim, because his next romance ended in marriage. He was introduced to high-flying Dr Beverly Marshall by his interfering and insufferable cousin Hilary. Beverly was going to be at a conference in Erinsborough and Hilary asked if Jim would take care of her for a few days.

Jim expected any friend of Hilary's to be awful, but was pleasantly surprised to find that Beverly enjoyed golf and fishing – and she was better at them than he was!

For a couple of years, Jim and Beverly enjoyed a happy marriage, but then Beverly became the third member of the Robinson family to change actor (she was originally played by Lisa Armytage), and Shaunna O'Grady's interpretation of the stressed doctor verged on the neurotic and seemed to get on Jim's nerves.

101

The break-up of the marriage was signalled early on when childless Beverly decided she wanted a baby of her own. The fact that she was guardian for her sister's children Todd and Katie Landers did not suppress her maternal cravings.

Jim was reluctant to become a father again, but was willing to try for a baby because it was clear that it meant the world to his wife. Even after a heart-breaking miscarriage, Beverly wasn't going to be deterred from motherhood and she investigated the option of adoption. And even when she learnt that Jim was too old to be accepted as an adoptive parent, she still would not relent in her obsessive quest for motherhood.

Another blow to the marriage came when Jim's business went bust in 1991, putting the onus on Beverly to be the breadwinner just when she wanted to stay at home.

Eventually, Beverly was allowed to foster baby Rhys, but when the boy was returned to his natural mother Beverly went off the rails and it signalled the death-knell in their marriage.

Over the years, Jim had a few medical scares, but the one that frightened him was a minor heart cramp suffered during a bike race. Superfit Jim was determined to fight the signs of ageing and was therefore thrilled when young and beautiful Caroline Alessi showed an interest in him in 1991.

The two embarked on a discreet affair but it didn't last long as too many of the neighbours disapproved. Jim's last romance before he died was with Annalise Hartman's mother, the scheming and beguiling Fiona.

Jim fell for the seductress – hook, line and sinker – without realising that she was trying to sink her talons into his bank account. Helen and Julie realised what a conniving bitch Fiona was and the friction between the three women took its toll on Jim, and in March 1994 he suffered a heart attack and died.

Fiona was with him at the time but instead of calling an ambulance she went to see Jim's stockbroker and cashed in his stocks. Later, she returned to the Robinson house with Rosemary where they 'discovered' Jim's body together.

It soon became clear that Fiona's story didn't add up and the viewers cheered when she was foiled and didn't get away with the deception. However, Helen and Julie never forgave her – or themselves – for being at war with kindly Jim when he died.

Jim's chequered love life is matched in ups and downs only by his elder son's. Paul Robinson has never had a problem in attracting women – but he's had a hellish time holding on to them!

After the disaster of his first marriage to Terri, Paul resolved to put business first – love, he said, was for suckers.

He found a platonic soul mate in Gail Lewis, a woman who had been his boss at the airline. When Paul found out that Gail had quit her life in the skies, he was quick to offer her the job as his Number Two at the Daniels Corporation.

Like Paul, Gail also had a disastrous marriage behind her to racing driver Jeremy Lord, and was equally happy to put work first to blot out her private life.

So when Paul realised the only way of clinching a lucrative property deal with an influential Japanese businessman was to get married – Mr Udugawa considered marriage to be a favourable indication of a man's judgement – Gail was quick to accept Paul's suggestion that they enter into a marriage of convenience.

They invited their relations round to Paul's house at Number 22 on the pretence that they were hosting a dinner party. But when Paul introduced his guests to the minister it was clear that the main course wouldn't be edible!

The Robinsons felt disappointed – they had been denied the chance for a major celebration – but Paul simply explained that they both wanted to keep it simple as they had both been married before. The truth was that there wasn't much to celebrate.

Paul and Gail worked closely together, and the Japanese contract that their marriage clinched meant they toiled long hours in the office. Family and friends thought their dedication to each other was touching, but sadly their dedication was only to their work.

When cousin Hilary stayed at Number 22 while she was in town for Scott and Charlene's wedding, she nearly blew Paul and Gail's cover when she spied that they were sleeping in separate rooms. However, an invented tale about an argument stopped any rumours spreading.

Slowly this pair developed a strong affection for each other, but because of the rules of their 'hands off' nuptials, neither could bring themselves to express their true feelings.

But a moment of elation after securing yet another deal led to a spontaneous kiss. Paul pulled back first and they both quickly apologised for getting out of hand.

The viewers were infuriated – everybody watching realised they were perfect for each other – but it would be another couple of months of crafty teasing before Scott finally made his brother say those three little words.

Just as Gail was about to walk out of Paul's life for good after admitting the marriage was a sham, Scott persuaded his big brother to go after Gail and tell her how he felt. They fell into each other's arms and quickly relocated to the same bedroom!

They both wanted to have children, but Gail had always known she was unable to conceive, and now that love was part of the equation she had to tell a disappointed Paul.

When Nina, an ex-girlfriend of Paul's from his airline days, arrived at Lassiter's with a toddler in tow, it didn't take long before it was revealed that Paul was little Amy's natural father. Gail panicked thinking this would mean Paul didn't want to have children with her, but her fear was unfounded and the couple tried every means possible to conceive.

After in vitro fertilisation treatment, the couple were told the joyous news that Gail was finally pregnant – with triplets!

Paul knew it would be a tough task to provide for his expected brood and became obsessive about making money. Gail was distraught that he had found yet more ways to worship the almighty dollar, and left him while she was pregnant realising that she would always be second best to Lassiter's.

Paul was upset but unrepentant and used it as an excuse to involve himself ever more deeply with his work. Naturally he couldn't run the business single-handed, and so he advertised for an assistant. The woman he appointed for the job was a beautiful young woman called Caroline Alessi, and Paul couldn't be quite sure that it wasn't her beauty that he was employing and not her CV! But when he discovered she had a twin sister, Christina, his confusion was resolved – he could date Chrissie while maintaining a professional relationship with her twin.

Chrissie was to be the third Mrs Paul Robinson, and the provider of Paul's fifth child – Andrew. But although Paul was well-versed in marriage vows, he still didn't know how to maintain a loving relationship without breaking hearts. And what he did to Chrissie was unbelievably cruel – he had an affair with her twin sister.

Caroline felt so guilty about the affair that she left Erinsborough to start over again in Italy. But Chrissie was so bemused by the hurried way Caroline left, that she demanded an explanation from Paul who finally confessed the dalliance.

Chrissie was heartbroken beyond comprehension – she had been stabbed in the back by the two people she loved most in the world – and it would take a superhuman effort for Paul to win back his wife and his son.

But he managed to convince Chrissie that he had never regretted anything quite so much in all his life, and his promise to never hurt her again led to the two of them reaffirming their marriage vows before leaving to start a new life together in Hawaii.

Julie returned to Ramsay Street in 1992 a completely different woman – literally. When she had left to care for injured Philip Martin who had been confined to a wheel chair she was played by Vikki Blanche.

But when the producers decided to bring back Julie, Vikki was in America and they decided to recast. She was replaced by the talented actress Julie

Mullins whose portrayal of Julie was so annoying that she quickly became one of the most hated characters on TV!

In her years away from Erinsborough, Julie had married kind-hearted Philip (who was now miraculously walking!) and had a daughter of her own, Hannah, as well as taking on the responsibility for Philip's children by his first wife, Loretta.

Philip's daughter Debbie became great friends with Julie, but his son Michael resented her so badly that he made her life hell.

But as Julie succeeded in annoying her family as much as she did her neighbours, it was only a matter of time before the marriage ran into difficulties.

No such problems arose for her little brother Scott who has stuck with the same woman since he was seventeen. He met and fell in love with girl-next-door Charlene Mitchell in 1987 and married her the following year. But although his love life was reasonably straightforward, his professional life didn't run quite so smoothly.

Although Scott never wanted to be anything other than a journalist, for a long time it looked like the closest he would get was doing the Erinsborough paper round – the newspapers were delivered by skateboard!

The first professional hiccup occurred when Scott flunked his all-important HSC (the Australian equivalent of A levels) because he was worried about Lucy who was missing at the time.

After his wedding he retook Year 12 and gained valuable work experience writing stories for the *Erinsborough News*. However, what he wrote was just a thinly veiled account of life in Ramsay Street and it was too obvious that 'Les and Daisy' were just literary replicas of Des and Daphne.

The neighbours were furious and Scott was forced to quit – and apologise to all those he'd offended. He finally got a chance to exercise his flair as a journalist when he graduated from high school a year later and joined the *Erinsborough News* as a cadet.

Scott was so committed to his profession that when his wife relocated to Brisbane he stayed behind for a few months until he could find an equivalent posiiton in Queensland.

His little sister Lucy went through about as many career changes as is possible for someone so young. Her original intention was to be a model, but then her dreams for the future varied from being an advertising executive to the next boss of Lassiter's before finally ending up as – ironically – a model!

Lucy changed actresses almost as frequently as she changed clothes. After Sasha Close steered the troubled lass through awkward puberty, the blonder Melissa Bell took Lucy into womanhood.

Lucy decided that she had had enough of her expensive boarding school and wanted to take her HSC at Erinsborough. It was an unexpected move, but Jim was over the moon to welcome back his youngest to the family nest.

But what he couldn't know was that another of his offspring was about to come and live with him. In 1991, Jim received a strange letter asking for financial assistance in paying for the funeral of a certain Maureen Donnelly.

Jim was flummoxed – he'd never heard of a Maureen Donnelly – and so he returned the letter explaining that the sender must have got the wrong person. But the sender was adamant and soon turned up on the doorstep of Number 26. His name was Glen and he claimed to be Jim's son.

It transpired that Jim had had a fling with Maureen while he was fighting in the Vietnam war, and unbeknown to him she had conceived. Glen thought it only right that as Jim had never paid any maintenance throughout his childhood, the least he could do was help out with Maureen's funeral expenses.

Jim was forced to concede and he tried to form a relationship with the son he never knew he had. It proved difficult as Glen was very proud and had a huge chip on his shoulder, but both men decided to give it a go and Glen moved into Number 26.

Paul did not take kindly to his half-brother and the two lads became bitter enemies. But Glen and Lucy felt an instant attraction, and it was all they could do to stop themselves from ending up in bed together. They kissed passionately (in a scene that was axed in the UK as the censors thought the incest storyline was too controversial) but stopped themselves from taking it any further.

Glen later became engaged to Gaby Willis, but he scrapped their marriage plans when he fell from the roof of The Waterhole and was paralysed. Glen had always been a physical man, and the loss of his legs caused a dramatic change in his character, and he deserted Ramsay Street a very unhappy man.

Lucy soon turned her attention to neighbour Brad Willis, but she had to fight for his love with country girl Beth Brennan. Lucy won her man and planned a future with Brad, but when she was offered a lucrative modelling contract in Singapore the lovers said a tearful farewell stating their intention to stay faithful.

Their hopes to stay together through the separation proved futile as Brad eventually got engaged to Beth, and Lucy fell in love and married in Singapore.

Lucy – and Melissa Bell – returned to Ramsay Street (as did Paul) for the special 2000th episode where she brought her new hubby home for inspection. Unfortunately, Jim didn't live long enough to see his youngest child married.

Thankfully though he died before his other daughter discovered that he was not in fact her father. Shortly after Jim's heart attack, Helen read some letters her daughter Anne had written to Jim in the early days of the marriage. What she read shocked her deeply – Jim was not Julie's dad.

Helen wrestled with her conscience and finally had to tell Julie what she knew. Julie went on a search to find her natural father, a man called Roger Bannon with whom it was thought Anne had had an affair.

Julie tracked down a Roger Bannon in Queensland, but was shocked to learn that he was only a couple of years older than her – he was Roger Bannon Jnr, her half-brother.

Julie was disgusted when he made a pass at her and sought out Roger Snr's wife, but was totally unprepared to hear the unfortunate and disturbing truth that she was the product of a rape – Anne had not had an affair at all. That story had simply been invented to protect her.

Julie returned to Ramsay Street in a preoccupied mood. She didn't reveal to anyone what she had learnt in Queensland, fearful that they would shun her if they knew of her brutal conception. She distanced herself from her husband and asked for a divorce.

However, Julie and Philip were to reunite for the 2000th episode where Philip reassured his estranged wife that he didn't care about the past – only the future.

THE WILLIS FAMILY

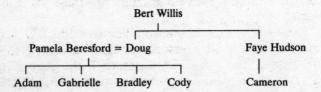

THE WILLIS FAMILY TREE

The first of this lively clan to make an appearance in *Neighbours* was fourteen-year-old Cody, who was at school with Todd, Josh and Melissa.

Occasionally she mentioned her family who had been going through a difficult time. Her parents Doug and Pam had recently separated causing grief for Cody and her siblings, Adam, Gaby and Brad. But Pam and Doug soon realised they missed each other madly and reconciled.

Pam and Doug married young after they met when she had been driving her father's taxi. Some pals of Doug's had played a joke on him leaving him naked in the street with only a bunch of flowers to preserve his modesty! Pam picked him up, and after she'd taken him home, Doug presented her with the bunch of flowers! She must have liked what she saw, because Pam and Doug are still together.

They are both enormously likeable people: Pam is

caring and capable, and Doug is warm-hearted and friendly. But because they both have formidable tempers they often find themselves having enormous 'blues'.

They bought Number 28 Ramsay Street from Des Clarke in 1990 and they moved in with their eldest son Adam, a 21-year-old medical student, and their youngest child, Cody.

Their other children Gaby, 17, and Brad, 16, were studying overseas at the time. But dealing with just two Willis kids proved enough for them to cope with!

Cody's main problem was her love life. At first she dated Josh Anderson, but later admitted that she was in love with his best mate Todd. In typical Cody style she made no bones about telling Todd how she felt: Cody had a way with words and her precocious and engaging manner coupled with her china-doll looks had men wrapped around her little finger – especially her dad.

But when Pam and Doug worried that perhaps Cody was seeing too much of her new boyfriend, they started laying down the law. The teenage sweethearts responded by running away in a bid to be together. However, their plan was foiled when Cody developed severe flu after sleeping in a barn and Todd was forced to take her home.

Adam's love life was slightly more complicated. First of all he fell for Caroline Alessi – or was it Christina? His inability to tell the twins apart caused him much grief, but he soon settled for Caroline, who got used to dates in his beat-up VW Beetle with his plastic medic's skeleton on the back seat!

What Adam and Caroline had going was little more than fun, but when Adam fell for another neighbour, Gemma Ramsay, it was a serious dose of the real thing.

Adam was also having a few confusions on the professional front. When his medical studies started to falter, he decided to do what Doug had always wanted him to do and join the family business. Doug was a self-employed builder who had always dreamed of passing on the family business to his eldest son.

But Doug had realised long ago that Adam didn't really want to be a builder, and so he decided to make Adam's days on the building site as miserable as possible. He took him on as little more than a skivvy and paid him peanuts. So it wasn't very surprising that Adam decided to return to medicine.

And when Gemma accepted a job at a wild life sanctuary in Newcastle, NSW, Adam arranged to study there too.

Cody was also thinking about leaving Erinsborough. Her principal Dorothy Burke had suggested that she might be capable of gaining a scholarship to study in America, and although Cody knew it meant leaving Todd behind, she also knew it was the chance of a lifetime.

Cody took the chance, and left behind the financial worries of her parents. Doug's construction firm had been feeling the pinch in the recession, and a last chance deal with Paul Robinson nearly crippled the Willises.

Paul and Doug made an odd couple in business with Paul in his flash designer suits and Doug, as always, in his shorts and T-shirt. But they both believed that a development of a guest house on Lassiter's ground was a dead cert for making money.

But when the costs started to spiral, Doug found

he had no way of putting up his share of the money. Pam's regular salary as a nurse at the local hospital (she had recently returned to work, much to her husband's consternation) was not going to keep them if the deal fell through, and at one point it seriously looked like they would have to sell the house.

The return of Gaby from her studies in Japan in 1992 to the family nest marked a turnaround in the family's fortunes. Not only was Gaby beautiful but she was also bright, and she conned one of Doug's clients into paying an overdue debt by pretending to be the family lawyer. It was the beginning of the end of their financial worries, and it meant the Willis family could stop counting every penny.

The only Willis yet to surface was Pam and Doug's second son Brad, who had been in California on a basketball scholarship. (When Scott Michaelson landed the part of Brad, the character was quickly changed from a basketball player to a surfer to make use of Scott's natural talent on the waves.)

As Pam and Doug looked forward to Brad's imminent return, news came through that Brad was being held in the fictional Asian country of Bagee on drugs trafficking charges.

Pam was at her wits' end knowing that the penalty, if Brad was found guilty, was death. Although they couldn't really afford it, Pam and Doug found the money to go to Bagee and see their son. Thankfully, a week or so later they brought Brad home to Ramsay Street where he appeared completely unphased by his ordeal.

In fact the first thing Brad did after a good night's sleep was drag neighbour Josh Anderson down to the beach for an early morning surf – it was clear Brad was a guy in touch with his priorities!

Brad was unlike any guy Ramsay Street had ever seen before. He was scruffy and aimless, and let's be honest, a bit dumb. But he was also terminally cute and he was never going to have any trouble attracting the girls.

Gaby meanwhile had ambition enough for the both of them and had opened up her own clothes boutique called Gabrielle in the Lassiter's complex. Gaby designed all the clothes herself and it looked like Gabrielle might be the first in a chain of shops.

Gaby's love life was also on course as she had started dating Jim Robinson's illegitimate son, Glen Donnelly – it seems to be a rule in Erinsborough that everyone must date someone from their own street!

Glen helped boost her business by encouraging Gaby to cash in on the famous name of one of her customers, Elizabeth Taylor. Of course this wasn't *the* Elizabeth Taylor, it was just a local resident, but the *Erinsborough News* picked up on the story and Gabrielle went from strength to strength. That was until Gaby's meddling aunt Faye accidentally started a fire in the boutique and Gaby lost everything.

She was about to lose her fiancé Glen too. He was fixing a banner on top of The Waterhole where he worked when he fell and was permanently paralysed. Deeply depressed and unable to deal with life in a wheelchair, Glen took off claiming that he couldn't inflict himself on Gaby now that he was paralysed. Gaby was heartbroken but put it to the back of her mind as she started her new job at the Robinson Corporation.

Brad meanwhile was having a little more luck in the love stakes – in fact he even had two women fighting over him! Lucy Robinson (now in her third incarnation as Melissa Bell) and a girl he'd met on holiday in Queensland, Beth Brennan. Both were quite happy to do battle for the privilege of kissing Ramsay Street's very own surf god!

In the end Lucy won, but when she left for a modelling career in Singapore, Beth seized her opportunity and muscled in on Brad, asking him to help her to lose her virginity.

Brad had by now developed his passion for surfing into something of a cottage industry by producing hand-made surfboards for mates and enthusiasts.

Although the lives of their children now seemed somewhat settled, Pam and Doug's marriage was facing its toughest test. When Doug appeared in the *Erinsborough News* in 1993, a woman called Jill Weir read the article and fell in love with him. Her absurd obsession with Doug verged on the psychotic, and she would stop at nothing to make him hers.

Jill's first plan of action involved becoming great pals with Pam, so great in fact that Pam even offered to put Jill up when she found herself temporarily homeless. When Doug returned from a trip to find Jill with her feet firmly under the table at Number 28 he was not best pleased.

He was well aware of Jill's intentions and felt threatened. But Pam was so concerned with her own closeness to Jim Robinson that she failed to notice what was happening. In fact it was Pam's relationship with Jim that had caused problems between Pam and Doug in the first place – and when Doug accused his wife of having an affair, Pam was affronted beyond belief.

Pam had fallen in love with Jim who pretty much felt the same way about her. However, there was no way that she would ever be unfaithful to Doug.

But Doug was about to cheat on her. While he was away on a conference Jill checked into the same hotel and seduced him. On his return to Erinsborough, Doug confessed his sin which Pam felt gave her licence to pursue Jim with vigour.

Although Gaby once caught her mother in a passionate embrace with Jim, their affair was never consummated because Jim felt he couldn't sleep with a mate's wife. Nevertheless, Doug and Pam remained at loggerheads until a boating accident several months later where Doug was lost at sea. Pam was so worried she was forced to confess that she still loved her husband, and when Doug was eventually brought to shore, they kissed and made up.

Gaby, like her parents, had also been in the love wars. Following Glen's desertion, she started seeing a string of men, most of whom Pam and Doug thought were unsuitable, including punk rocker Zed.

But when Simon Hunter, a client of hers at the Robinson Corporation (and who had previously dated Melanie Pearson) asked her out, Gaby – and her parents – thought she'd found Mr Right.

But when Simon took Gaby away for a weekend he tried to rape her. Gaby returned to Erinsborough and tearfully told her mother what had happened. Doug reacted by thumping Simon who had turned into a slimy man willing to do anything to protect his own neck. So when Gaby announced that she was going to tell the police, Simon retorted that he would accuse Doug of assault. Although Doug was more than willing to cop an assault conviction if it meant bringing Simon to justice, Gaby decided she wanted to put the whole mess behind her and all the charges were dropped. Naturally, it was a long time before Gaby started seeing men again, but when school teacher Wayne Duncan arrived in Erinsborough there was an instant attraction.

However, that's about all there was and whenever they were together they fought like cat and dog. Gaby would much rather have an intimate dinner at an exclusive restaurant and go to the theatre, Wayne would rather gobble up some bush tucker while taking in a strenuous walk in the forest!

They would have probably never given their relationship serious consideration had it not been for Gaby's grandfather Bert Willis. Doug had not spoken to his father for decades and he was unaware that Gaby had been writing to Bert in secret for years. Towards the end of 1993, Gaby – with Pam's blessing – asked Bert to come and stay with them at Number 28.

Bert came and there was instant friction between him and Doug who had never forgiven his father for deserting his mother while he was still a kid. Bert did his best to explain himself, but Doug was not about to forgive him. It was only when Bert revealed to Wayne that he was dying that his behaviour made sense – he had come to Erinsborough to make amends before he passed away. Wayne eventually had to break his promise of silence to Bert because he could see that Doug would never give him a chance otherwise.

But Bert didn't want his son's pity and made plans to leave on the next boat (old sailors die hard), but Pam drove to the dock and persuaded Bert to come ashore for a last ditch effort at a reunion with his son.

It worked! Bert was so grateful to Wayne for

playing his part that he told Gaby it was his dying wish that she and Wayne get it together.

However, Gaby and Wayne still fought like children and it was going to be a stormy relationship. Nevertheless, they battled it out for a couple of months in the face of Pam's disapproval (she found Wayne's right-wing views uncompromisingly selfish), but when Gaby failed to stand by Wayne when he was accused of murder, Wayne ended their affair.

Brad meanwhile was starting an affair. Although he and Beth were now in love and engaged (with a wedding planned for the very near future), when he met a mystery woman riding a horse on the beach there was an instant attraction. They had a brief conversation before Brad got back to his surfing, and even though they hadn't even got each other's names, Brad somehow felt that they were going to be together.

So you can imagine his surprise when the same woman rode her horse into Ramsay Street the next day and revealed herself to be Lou Carpenter's daughter!

Brad's dilemma was made worse when Lauren Carpenter and Beth became good friends and the three of them had to spend a lot of time together. Lauren and Brad tried to deny their lust so as not to hurt Beth who had immersed herself in extravagant wedding plans.

But one day in March 1994 when they found themselves alone on the beach, Brad and Lauren finally made love. Back in Ramsay Street they went to even greater lengths to avoid each other so as not to be caught out.

But on the morning of his wedding, Beth caught him talking to Lauren on the beach. Beth later quizzed Lauren about the encounter and Lauren denied she had been at the beach, giving Beth the proof she needed to confirm her suspicions that Brad had someone else.

Still, it was too late to back out of the wedding now and so Beth went through with the charade of putting on her wedding dress and going to the ceremony. But she couldn't help noticing that Brad was staring at Lauren, and so when it was Beth's turn to say her vows, she backed out at the last minute and called the marriage off.

This gave Brad the chance to see Lauren, although out of deference to Beth – who was still in love with him – they kept their liaisons secret. But when Gaby was showing Number 22 to potential tenants, she caught the illicit lovers redhanded! (Brad had stolen the key so that he and Lauren could have some privacy.)

Their secret was out, but the affair was short-lived. Like Gaby and Wayne, the attraction had been almost entirely physical, and eventually Brad and Lauren called it quits, leaving Brad free to marry Beth.

Gaby had long since put love on the back burner and was concentrating on her burgeoning career at Lassiter's. She often clashed with her boss Philip Martin who she felt could always do better.

She set out to prove this by putting Lassiter's on a cost-cutting drive – an endeavour that attracted more customers. Paul Robinson – who was now based in Hawaii – noticed Gaby's efforts and when he returned to Erinsborough for Helen's birthday (and the show's 2000th episode) in the summer of 1994, he made Gaby the new boss of Lassiter's.

WAIFS AND STRAYS

Although *Neighbours* is very much a show based around families, over the years several orphans and lost souls have found a friend and a roof over their heads in Ramsay Street.

JOSH ANDERSON

A school friend of Todd Landers, Jim Robinson's nephew, Josh was often seen hanging around in Ramsay Street with Todd and their girlfriends Melissa Jarrett and Cody Willis.

But it wasn't until his parents' newsagent's shop was burnt down and the Anderson family moved to the country to make a new start, that Josh became a Ramsay Street regular.

He was very academic and unwilling to leave his studies at Erinsborough High. Luckily for him, Jim Robinson agreed to take him in as a lodger.

Josh and Jim became very close as finally Jim had found someone to follow in his footsteps. Paul, Scott and Todd had all turned their backs on engineering, but in Josh, Jim saw the protégé he had always hoped for. In fact at times Todd felt quite out of place when Josh and Jim got together.

Josh's good looks meant he never had any problems with the girls and he dated Cody Willis for a time. He later dated her friend Melissa Jarrett, but their relationship hit the rocks when he started seeing the mysterious Katrina.

Josh regularly bragged that he had something going with an older woman. Naturally, Melissa became jealous and she followed him to find out who Katrina really was. It turned out that Josh's mystery woman was in fact his violin teacher who he had a crush on!

To provide himself with a little extra money, Josh took the unusual career move of becoming a stripper! Encouraged by Melanie Pearson, he started working for an agency that generally booked him for hen parties. And when he was booked for Helen Daniels' hen party he had no choice but to perform.

However, the girls were so impressed with him that they ripped off the mask that maintained his anonymity. He was mortified, although his embarrassment gradually dispersed when the guests at Helen's party made him realise he should be proud of his body and not ashamed.

Nevertheless, it was clear to Josh that he wasn't doing a very good job of supporting himself, and he agreed to return to his parents where he would study for a career in computers, a field in which he was something of an expert.

In fact, Josh's computer flair frequently got him into trouble, like the time when he amended Todd's exam results on the school computer, or organised a homework service for his fellow pupils.

But once his skill proved to be a lifesaver, when he rescued the entire Lassiter's files after the system was crippled by a virus. He even managed to bring a smile to Paul Robinson's face!

BOUNCER

Perhaps the most loved neighbour of all, Bouncer the labrador was taken in by almost all of Ramsay Street's households.

He was originally the pet of Mike Young, but the lovable dog took pity on lonely Mrs Mangel and chose to go and live with her – much to Mike's dismay.

He stayed with the Mangel family after Nell left for a new life in England, first with Joe and then with Toby.

Bouncer's life in Ramsay Street was as varied as any other resident: he was run over by Madge Bishop when she was learning to drive; he became a hero when he answered the phone when baby Sky was in trouble; he even got married!

Yes, it was possibly the only dog marriage in soap history, but when Bouncer fell head over paw for Clarrie McLachlan's sheepdog Rosie, he married her in his dreams. Bouncer was so 'human' that no one dared laugh at the suggestion that he had dreams!

In real life, Bouncer was trained by an animal agency called Luke's Canine Actors, and Bouncer was as loved in reality as he was on screen. So when he got ill in 1992 he was allowed time to recuperate. Sadly, Bouncer was not to recover from his cancer, but he did return to Ramsay Street for one final storyline where he fathered a litter of puppies in neighbouring Anson's Corner. He died in 1993 aged seven.

Beth and her brother David first met their Ramsay Street pals while on holiday in the Australian resort of Surfers' Paradise. Brad, Lucy and Josh had all taken the trip north to get in some sun and sea, and they ended up hanging out with David and Beth.

But the holiday wasn't just fun. It turned out that David, and especially Beth, had had more than a few problems with their mother's lover.

Her mum Phyllis, or Bunny as she was known, was a real country girl who had married Beth's dad Bill when she was 22. The couple had a happy marriage until tragedy struck and Bill was killed when his tractor rolled over and crushed him.

Following Bill's death, Bunny worked hard to raise her kids and run the farm, and so she was quite surprised to find herself taking a lover. She had no idea that her fancy man had designs on Beth, so when Bunny discovered that he had been interfering with her daughter she turfed him out, and Beth and David took that trip to Surfers' Paradise.

Lucy was so upset to hear about what had happened to her new friend that she invited Beth to come and stay with them in Ramsay Street if things ever got tough at home again.

Beth would have followed Lucy back to Ramsay Street immediately if it hadn't been for her brother's pleadings, but eventually David let her go and Beth soon knocked on the door of Number 26.

Lucy was thrilled to have her pal come to stay, but less thrilled when she realised Beth also had her eye on Brad – just like she did!

The two girls entered an absurd battle for Brad,

who loved the attention of being in the middle of Ramsay Street's hottest love triangle for years. Lucy eventually won Brad's affection, but Beth had already found a replacement, a guy called Rod Baker.

The neighbours were desperate to meet the mysterious Rod, and when he arrived they realised why Beth had been so cagey about talking about him – he was twice her age. Beth refused to listen to her friends' words of counsel and continued to date him, and when he proposed she accepted without hesitation. There was just one problem – sex. After what had happened with her mum's boyfriend, Beth was reluctant to get intimate with a man, and this reluctance led to Rod breaking off their engagement.

Lucy persuaded Beth that she had done the right thing in saying 'no' and waiting until she was ready, but Beth thought it was time she grew up.

So when Lucy left for a new career in Singapore, Beth once again became interested in Brad. She wasn't looking for a relationship though, she was just looking for some experience. So, bold as brass, she just came out with it and asked Brad to sleep with her!

He was too shocked to say yes and so instead he turned her down. But one night, while they were left alone in the unfinished Lassiter's guest house waiting for a goods delivery, Brad finally agreed to help Beth overcome her fears and they made love.

Although it was unintentional, Brad and Beth found themselves drawn into a relationship. They had already become good friends as Beth was a labourer for Willis Constructions (Brad's father's company) where she endured many jibes and sexist remarks from men in the industry, but Doug – encouraged by Brad – always backed her up.

Brad was genuinely fond of Beth and gave her a friendship ring to express the way he felt. But Beth misinterpreted his feelings and took the ring to be of the engagement variety, and when Brad saw how happy she was he didn't have the heart to tell her the truth.

So an excited Beth started making plans for her wedding. Gaby designed and fitted her for a dress, and Phoebe was to be her bridesmaid as was Lauren, Brad's other woman.

Beth had no idea that Brad was crazy for Lauren; if she had it would have broken her heart. In fact it wasn't until the morning of her wedding that Beth spotted the clandestine lovers together on the beach. Suddenly the pieces began to fit into place, especially when Lauren denied that she had even been on the beach. But Beth still felt she didn't have enough evidence to call off the wedding.

So she got into her dress and made her way to the outdoor service. It was only when she walked down the aisle that Beth got the evidence she needed as Brad and Lauren couldn't take their eyes off each other. Beth blanched when it was her turn to take her vows and her planned future with Brad crumbled instantly.

Naturally, Beth took a week or so away from Ramsay Street to come to terms with Brad's betrayal, but on her return to Erinsborough she still believed that she and Brad were meant to be together. Brad meanwhile had started dating Lauren quite openly and it was clear Beth was no longer the one Brad wanted.

Although she dated chef Harvey half-heartedly and

tried to concentrate on her career when Doug Willis had to sell his company to Constructorcon, Beth still carried a torch for Brad. But it was only when Lucy Robinson arrived back in town for her grandmother's birthday that Brad realised he still had feelings for Beth too.

He had since split with Lauren after they rowed too often over his gambling, leaving him free. Ironically it was Lucy – the one Beth had originally fought with for Brad – that made Brad see Beth was the girl for him by telling him a few home truths.

The reunited lovers again made plans for a future together, and this time it looks like they'll be together forever.

EDDIE BUCKINGHAM

Eddie was quite a milestone creation for the *Neighbours* bosses, for not only was he English, but he was also black. And in the snow-white suburb of Erinsborough, Eddie was always going to stand out from the crowd.

A happy-go-lucky chap, he followed Madge and Harold Bishop to Australia after they had met him during a trip to England. He had worked in a café that they had frequented, and in exchange for handy tourist tips on London, they whetted Eddie's wanderlust with tales of Australia.

They had become such good friends that when the Bishops took their return flight Down Under they extended to Eddie an invitation to visit – they would also be able to give him work in the Coffee Shop which Harold now owned.

What Madge and Harold didn't expect was for

Eddie to turn up on their doorstep only days after getting home themselves. But nevertheless, they rented jovial Eddie a room and gave him work as promised.

Everybody loved Eddie. He was a good source of gossip, advice and outrageous stories about his days on the road. But the storyliners failed to find him any convincing plots, and it wasn't long before he was shipped back to Blighty where his father had been taken ill.

DOROTHY BURKE

All the pupils at Erinsborough High were scared of their formidable principal Dorothy Burke when they first met her, but a closer inspection revealed Dorothy possessed a crafty sense of humour.

She was an intensely private person, and the neighbours wondered about her past when she first moved into Number 30. All they knew was that she was well educated and well travelled (her living room was decorated with tribal masks and souvenirs from a lifetime of exotic trips). It was only when Toby Mangel became friendly with Dorothy's niece Lochy that Dorothy's life began to unfold for the neighbours.

Her nephew Ryan also came to stay, and Dorothy showed that she had no experience in raising children when she failed to keep the brooding youth under control.

But the neighbours – especially Madge who had become a great rival of Dorothy's – still wondered about the mysterious Mr Burke whom she never mentioned.

The picture started to develop when Ryan found

a letter from Dorothy's husband Colin with words cut out of the paper. He realised that this is how prison officers control their inmates' letters, and confronted his aunt with the theory that Colin was in prison.

Much to her shame, Dorothy had to confess Ryan was right. Colin had been convicted of fraud when he was an accountant. On his release from prison, Colin persuaded Dorothy to take him back, but it was only a matter of weeks before she lived to regret listening to her no good husband.

It was Joe Mangel who first found out Colin was cheating on his wife again. While he was cleaning the windows at Lassiter's, he spied Colin in a compromising position with Helen's high flying daughter Rosemary Daniels.

Rosemary had no idea Colin was married, but Dorothy wasn't interested in blaming her anyway – it was Colin she wanted to seek revenge on. She threw him out and made sure he never returned to Ramsay Street. Nevertheless, the embarrassment of what her husband had done stayed with her for a very long time and she gave up any hope of finding love again.

When Lochy returned to her parents and Ryan joined the army, Dorothy's house was not empty for long. She took in her star pupil Phoebe Bright following the death of her father, and Toby Mangel when his dad went to live in Europe.

They made an unusual family but it worked. Both Toby and Phoebe respected Dorothy, and she enjoyed taking care of such responsible young people.

Dorothy's feud with Madge peaked when they both ran for local council. Dorothy was determined to win a seat on the council so she could fight the proposed plans to close down Erinsborough High. The two women were forced to call a temporary truce when they were trapped in the ladies' toilets together overnight at the end of a campaign function.

Dorothy's severe looks, bold dress sense (she often wore an imposing black hat and was never seen without her parasol in summer) and haughty sense of humour made her many enemies, but for some they were an attraction.

When she met education inspector Tom Merrick in 1993 there was an instant chemistry, even though he was several years her junior.

Although she tried to deny that she felt anything for a long time, in the end she finally had to let her heart rule her unsentimental head for the first time. She threw caution to the wind for the first time in years, and quite literally rode off into the sunset with Tom and Toby on the back of Tom's motorbike for a new life in the country.

BRONWYN DAVIES

After the death of his wife, Daphne, Des Clarke found it hard to cope as a working single parent, and he advertised for a nanny for his son Jamie.

But before Des found the right person for the job, he had to combine the roles of bank manager, homemaker and daddy all at once. During one flustered trip to the supermarket, Des's stressed state nearly caused catastrophe. He took his groceries back to his car and while he was loading his shopping and coping with a folding pushchair he lost sight of toddler Jamie for just a few seconds. But that's all it took.

In a state of panic, Des searched the car park calling out his son's name. Eventually the little tot ran into the arms of a pretty blonde teenage girl who was holding him when Des finally found his son.

The girl told Des he was an unfit father and it was criminal that someone so uncaring had such a beautiful child.

Des thanked the girl for her insults before taking Jamie back to Number 28 where he had a string of nanny applicants to interview.

The first candidate through the door was none other than the girl from the car park – Bronwyn Davies. Des and Bronwyn decided to put their bad start behind them and try again, and so Bronwyn moved in with the Clarkes.

Bronwyn was a country girl with a big heart who had tired of life on the farm and come to the big smoke in search of adventure. She certainly found it in Ramsay Street!

Bronwyn fell for *Neighbours*' joker in the pack, Henry Ramsay and the pair embarked on a very serious love affair. Bronny was distracted from her romance by the arrival of her younger sister Sharon who turned up out of the blue and announced she was staying.

The sisters had quite a fiery relationship – Sharon had her head in the clouds and Bronwyn always had to bring her down to earth – but when the chips were down they stuck together.

The sisters moved in with Mrs Mangel as her lodgers, but it wasn't long before Bronwyn was on the move again. Her relationship with Henry was now very serious and the lovers took the important decision to move in with each other.

But unlike Henry's younger sister Charlene, the couple didn't feel the need to tie the knot first. They convinced Henry's mum Madge that the idea of 'living in sin' was very old-fashioned, and so she let them share a room at Number 24. (The truth was Madge missed Charlene terribly, and she was more than pleased to have sensible Bronwyn as a surrogate daughter.)

Bronwyn had since left behind the care of children and had embarked on her training to become a vet. But when her now fiancé Henry was offered a radio DJ's job in New Zealand, Bronwyn had to choose between her job and going with Henry.

She elected to stay on in Erinsborough until she could find equivalent work in New Zealand. That meant saying a temporary goodbye to Henry, but living with his mum made the separation more bearable as they could both talk about him without boring each other!

But sure enough, a couple of months later, Bronwyn followed Henry to New Zealand where they later married.

ZOE DAVIS

Zoe was one of the wildest and most unconventional women Erinsborough ever knew. Her devil-may-care attitude to money, trouble and inconvenience made her at once charming and infuriating as she blazed a trail of confusion and amusement through everybody else's lives.

She was a high-school friend of Daphne Lawrence

and she came to Erinsborough for her pal's wedding to Des Clarke. She house-sat for the newlyweds while they were on honeymoon and soon set about sinking her claws into Ramsay Street.

First of all she became one of many cast regulars to be Paul's secretary. Zoe had many careers – as a singer, dancer, saleswoman and waitress – and sometimes she did some of these jobs at the same time. She took all of her careers very seriously but just couldn't decide between them! Then Zoe started looking for love which she found at Number 26 in the shape of an older man, Jim Robinson.

Unsurprisingly, the Robinsons – especially nine-year-old Lucy – were disdainful of Jim dating a woman twenty years his junior. However, against the odds, Jim and Zoe made a go of their relationship only for things to take an unexpected turn when Zoe announced she was pregnant.

Jim was reluctant to become a father again in his mid-forties and he and Zoe became distant when she insisted on keeping the baby. She was happy being pregnant – perhaps now she could stop flitting around from ambition to ambition.

But one day when she was alone at Number 28, she was crippled by a searing pain in her abdomen and collapsed unconscious on the floor.

For a while it looked like she would not be found before it was too late, but just in the nick of time she was rushed to hospital where it was diagnosed that she had suffered a ectopic pregnancy and had miscarried.

In typical Zoe fashion she said, 'Never mind, I can always have another baby.' But Daphne had to break the news to her that she would probably never be able to conceive. Even this piece of news Zoe managed to take well. She simply picked herself up and moved on to the next plan.

In an effort to distance herself from the disappointment of the pregnancy, Zoe took off but she returned undaunted to Erinsborough the following year – but this time she had a man in tow.

Tony Chapman was as mad as she was and it was hard to see how they would ever manage their finances or find enough responsibility between them to rent an apartment and remember to visit the supermarket.

Zoe's madcap ways meant she didn't care for keeping track of her finances, and Des had to break the news to her that the bank was withdrawing her finances. Naturally, Zoe didn't register that this was particularly important and almost merrily took the scissors to her plastic, only to discover in the following days that she was really broke.

But Tony came to the rescue and proposed marriage. Although this was absolutely no guarantee of financial security, getting married seemed like fun. And anyway, Zoe had never had a wedding before!

Although Ramsay Street never heard from her again, none of the neighbours doubted that she would ever change!

WAYNE DUNCAN

Erinsborough High's arrogant chemistry teacher got off to a bad start in Ramsay Street. When he knocked on the door of Number 26 in 1993, Jim assumed he was another of the phoney buyers the neighbours had arranged to stop him from selling the house. Wayne waited patiently for Jim to stop berating him before calmly announcing that he had come to visit Helen.

Wayne was the son of Helen's cousin Thelma, and as he was moving to the area he thought he'd look up his long lost relatives. Jim repaired the damage by asking Wayne to stay with them.

Wayne also got off to a bad start with most of his new associates, especially those he taught like Debbie and Rick. He got into further strife with his pupils when the vixen-like Annalise spread rumours that the two of them were having an affair. Even though this wasn't true, everyone was ready to believe her as Wayne had been forced out of his last job because of similar gossip.

The person Wayne created the most amount of friction with was Gaby Willis. They got off to a terrible start when she tipped a glass of beer over him! She thought he was arrogant and he thought she was precocious. But their harsh words concealed an undeniable passion.

Wayne and Gaby were like chalk and cheese. He liked sport. She hated it. He liked going for walks in the country. She liked going to the theatre. But one way or another these two were determined to date.

However, every time they went out they ended up fighting like cat and dog. They agreed to call a truce, and Gaby invited Wayne round to Number 28 for dinner with her parents. Needless to say it was a total disaster and Wayne ended up arguing with Pam about politics!

But then Wayne loves a good argument. He's articulate and intelligent, and a good match for anyone willing to take their chances. And Pam was ready for battle. She couldn't believe that he owned a gun and kept it at Jim's house. She was outraged when he said he would shoot a burglar. Wayne tried to explain that being brought up in the macho environment of a small country town had made him very protective of his 'patch', but Pam still thought his attitudes were unforgivable.

Wayne was generally a lucky man, but his luck ran out one night in April 1993 when a gang of bikers mistook him for the Gottliebs' lodger Russell and beat him up and left him for dead.

He went back to his parents' farm to recuperate after the attack. When he returned he was arrested for the murder of the biker leader Cactus who had been found shot dead.

Many of the neighbours believed Wayne was more than capable of such a revenge attack, but when even Gaby showed that she doubted him, he knew he had to prove his own innocence.

But it was an uphill struggle as an eye-witness had picked him out from a line-up and confirmed he had been at the scene of the murder.

Wayne managed to persuade the witness, an old lady with a poor memory, that she had got her dates confused when he told her he remembered she had been carrying an umbrella. She conceded that the murder had taken place on a sunny day and withdrew her testimony.

However, not all the neighbours were entirely convinced of Wayne's innocence, and he had much to do before the school would reinstate him after suspending him. But there was nothing Gaby could do to win him back as he never forgave her for not believing in him.

Eccentric Clive raised a few eyebrows when he first took up residence at Number 22. For the first few weeks all the other residents of Ramsay Street saw of their new neighbour was his brightly painted car in the driveway, and lots of men in gorilla suits coming and going!

Everything was soon explained when it was revealed that red-haired Clive ran a gorilla-gram message service.

Many of the Ramsay Streeters saw Clive as simply a fool with a way with words. But when young Lucy Robinson stumbled into the Robinsons' kitchen while Clive had popped in for a chat, he quickly became a hero. Lucy had had an allergic reaction to a bee sting and her air passage had swollen up so badly that she could hardly breathe.

Clive took charge of the situation and demanded that Helen bring him hot water and a sharp knife. In a state of panic Helen did as she was told and only later did she ask what Clive wanted them for.

'Trust me,' he said. 'I'm a doctor.' And there on the kitchen table he performed a tracheotomy on the young girl to open up her air passage. If he'd waited for the ambulance to arrive, Lucy would have certainly died. People were so amazed to realise that there was so much more to Clive than a series of silly one-liners that it took them a while to start questioning why he wasn't practising medicine any more.

But eventually they did start asking questions. Clive managed to avoid giving direct answers, but it was clear that he was hiding a painful secret. So in the face of everyone's suggestions that he return to medicine, Clive simply hardened his resolve not to and expanded his gimmick empire.

The first plan was Gift of the Gab. Aware that he had a talent for being able to say the things other people shied away from, Clive saw a gap in the market for a service that would dare to say what everyone else was keeping to themselves.

Whether it was telling Mrs Mangel she was a grouchy old bag, or proposing to your loved one in an unusual way, Clive Gibbons was at your service. For a small fee, Clive would gladly undertake your dirty work and get your message across with style.

His most noted successes included reuniting Dan and Edna Ramsay, as well as Des and Daphne even though, like every other man in Ramsay Street, he had fallen in love with Des's bride.

Together with Shane Ramsay, Clive ventured into the gardening business when the two friends formed RAGGS (Ramsay and Gibbons Gardening Services) which proved rather lucrative for the young men.

But the arrival of his brother Graham, his wife and daughter Vicky, almost put paid to Clive's various careers. Like his brother, Graham was also a qualified doctor, and because he was happy doing what he was doing, Graham couldn't understand why his little brother had given up on medicine.

Clive was backed into a corner and he was forced to reveal that he had once made an error in medical judgement which had led to the death of his then girlfriend. It seemed all the pranks and jollity since had been a successful way of covering up his grief and pain.

Graham tried to persuade Clive to return to medicine, and it took plenty of explaining to understand that Clive was truly happy the way he was.

And he was about to get happier. Susan Cole, the mother of Charlene and Henry's half-brother Sam, found herself homeless, and Clive readily offered to take them in. He was a natural with baby Sam and Susan really couldn't imagine what she'd done to earn Clive's friendship and kindness. Just when she was about to get depressed about being an unemployed single mum, Clive would tell her a joke and offer to babysit while she went for a job interview.

You see, Clive had fallen in love with Susan and her young son, but he was such a gentleman that he would never dream of making a move on her while she was dependent on him for a place to live – he didn't want her to feel compromised.

If only he'd been able to use the services of Gift of the Gab for himself! For this was the one occasion that had Clive truly tongue-tied.

Eventually, the message finally got through to Susan but she had already fallen for Paul Robinson. Clive couldn't understand that Susan would prefer Paul, and even though she eventually rejected Paul as well, he decided to throw himself back into medicine and took up a GP's position in an adjacent borough.

Clive was not quickly forgotten in Ramsay Street as he gave Bertha, his car, to Henry Ramsay (Bertha would later be passed on to Scott for his honeymoon, and eventually to Matt Robinson), who also took over Clive's gardening round.

ANNALISE HARTMAN

When Annalise offered herself to 50-year-old Lou Carpenter he couldn't believe his luck! She was a vision of loveliness with her cascading blonde hair and pink hot pants. Lou was so smitten that he even proposed to her, but he quickly withdrew his offer when her mother arrived and informed him Annalise was only seventeen.

Annalise made a habit out of using men for their money and fooling people that she was a lot older than she was (Lou believed her to be 21). She even defrauded Lassiter's by checking in as a guest with no intention of paying her bills. (In the end she had to work off her debt by becoming a chamber maid.)

Annalise was a pretty mixed-up kid who grew up without her father (her mother Fiona always told her he had died when she was little, but it later turned out that Fiona had walked out on him), and with only Fiona as a role model, Annalise learnt to wrap men around her little finger.

She also followed Fiona into the hairdressing business for a while, as she saw hairdressing to be a glamorous profession. Annalise was obsessed with her looks and her clothes, and was never seen without her make-up. Even so, she still found a good friend in the more down-to-earth Beth Brennan. But for some reason she made an enemy of Gaby Willis and the two women often had bitchy cat fights.

She wasn't very lucky in love. After Lou she dated a string of no-hopers including Russell Butler and chef Harvey Johnson. But it was with Harvey's replacement at Lassiter's, that Annalise finally found a lover worth making a fuss over.

He was Mark Gottlieb who was almost as much of a flirt as she was! But the real pleasure in dating Mark came from the knowledge that she had beaten Gaby Willis in the race to capture him!

Although technically part of the Willis clan (his outrageous mother Faye is Doug's sister), Cameron was a bit of a misfit in Ramsay Street.

A lawyer by profession, Cameron was already doubtful about his chosen career by the time he first set foot in Erinsborough. But there was plenty of legal work for him defending his aunt Pam against a murder charge following the death of Garth Kirby, an old friend of the family.

But he soon jacked it in and looked around for alternatives. One of his most unusual jobs was writing erotic fiction, for which he found an unexpected collaborator in Helen Daniels.

He found romance in Ramsay Street with an ex-client of his, the sophisticated Jacqueline Summers, and then with Lauren Carpenter, who would eventually break his heart. But first a local villain, Gavin Heywood, would try to break his back.

Cameron was blackmailed into becoming Heywood's lawyer, but when he'd learnt too much about Heywood's underworld dealings it was soon made clear that he would be made to keep silent – permanently.

The only way Cameron could free himself from Heywood's clutches was to get some information on the crook that he could bargain with. And so Cameron managed to save his own life, but only by the skin of his teeth.

Cameron eventually left town when he realised that Lauren Carpenter had been using him to keep her mind off Brad Willis, the man she was really in love with. But he no longer needed her to boost his confidence, as he had just plucked up the courage to try his hand as a stand-up comedian. He left Erinsborough to pursue his art.

TODD LANDERS

Just when it seemed that Jim Robinson's wedding to Dr Beverly Marshall would be an unusually idyllic and uncomplicated affair, Beverly's nephew and niece, Todd and Katie Landers, decided to run away.

It seemed that they were worried about what their violent father Bob would do to their mum (Bev's sister Annette) while they were away. It was arranged for the two kids to stay at the Robinsons while Beverly returned to Adelaide to check on her sister.

The outcome was that Beverly thought the kids would be better off staying in Ramsay Street until their parents had sorted out their difficulties.

Surprisingly, Jim seemed quite happy for Todd and Katie to stay. Apparently enjoying a honeymoon period alone with his wife wasn't high on his list of priorities.

The kids enrolled at Erinsborough High, where Todd quickly showed his aptitude for academia and girls! He started dating local girl Melissa Jarrett, and his best friend Josh Anderson went out with precocious Cody Willis.

However, Cody would much rather have been dating Todd and Josh secretly had his eye on Melissa! So when Josh and Mel finally got their act together, Cody was quick to provide Todd with a shoulder to cry on. They went out to Lassiter's lake for a heart-to-heart where Cody stunned Todd with

143

the news that she was in love with him (something the viewers had known for weeks).

The teenagers embraced and sealed their new romance with an awkward kiss. It was the start of a very serious relationship for two people so young, and when Cody's parents, Pam and Doug, moved into Ramsay Street they realised that Cody and Todd were probably seeing too much of each other.

But their attempts to split them up largely failed – after all, they would always see each other at school. However, Pam and Doug feared that her romance with Todd would seriously jeopardise Cody's academic capabilities and they laid down the law to the young lovers. They were to stop seeing each other until the exams were over, and if they still wanted to be together after the tests then Pam and Doug would not stand in their way.

But the Willis' plan backfired in a big way. Todd and Cody decided to run away in a bid to be together. For weeks they were missing from Ramsay Street and no one heard from them.

Pam and Doug and Beverly and Jim were distraught, but Todd and Cody were just happy to be together. They had gone off into the country where Todd had found himself a poorly paid job on a farm. They couldn't afford rent and so they slept rough in a barn. But the cold nights and poor nutrition soon took their toll on the delicate Cody and she contracted severe flu.

She was so ill that Todd had to concede that they couldn't make it alone and took her home via the hospital.

The only way Pam and Doug managed to keep Todd and Cody apart was by encouraging her to take the opportunity of studying on scholarship in America.

When she left, Todd vowed to stay faithful to her. So when a letter arrived from Cody a few months later saying she had met someone else he was devastated. Thankfully, his pal Josh had now moved in with him at the Robinsons' and the two lads amused themselves with bouts of computer hacking and rigging exam results.

Josh had fallen for Phoebe Bright at school as she was just about the only person there brighter than him. But yet again, the two friends were about to swap girlfriends.

Todd understood Phoebe better than Josh and she recognised that. Like Phoebe, Todd had also gone through the ugly duckling stage of wearing braces and growing his hair out of that 'awkward' stage. Todd realised Phoebe's potential and knew that when he removed her geeky glasses he would find the woman of his dreams.

Phoebe and Todd's relationship took a serious turn when they decided to sleep with each other. Although they discussed their emotions and feelings they forgot to talk about contraception and Phoebe fell pregnant.

The couple talked over their expectant state with their respective guardians Jim Robinson and Dorothy Burke, and they decided that the best thing for everybody would be if Phoebe had an abortion, even though they themselves would have liked to have become parents.

So Phoebe went to the abortion clinic and prepared for her operation. Meanwhile, back in Ramsay Street, Todd had decided that he definitely wanted to keep the baby. He rushed out of Number 26 and leapt on a bus to the clinic aware that it was a race against the anaesthetist's watch.

But the traffic was lousy and so he jumped off the bus and decided to press ahead on foot. But to go in the right direction he had to cross a busy road. In his desperation he failed to see an oncoming van and he was knocked down.

His body went into a series of convulsions and it looked like he might die, but he knew he had to live to save his unborn child. The paramedics arrived and rushed him to casualty where someone contacted the Robinsons. Mercifully, the Robinsons contacted the clinic where Phoebe was due for her termination, and the message got there just in time.

Phoebe and Dorothy rushed to Todd's bedside where his condition seemed to have stabilised. When he regained consciousness Phoebe was waiting at his side. Todd assumed that Phoebe had already had the abortion and was overjoyed to find out the message had got to her in time. But just as they were going to start making plans for the future, Todd suffered a massive heart attack and died.

But that was not Todd's last appearance in *Neighbours*. Shortly after his dramatic funeral, at which his dad Bob held Helen Daniels at gun point, Phoebe saw Todd come to her in a vision. He told her not to worry as he would take care of her and their daughter.

Although Phoebe was sure that her eyes weren't deceiving her, it was only when she finally gave birth to a little girl she knew Todd had really been watching over her.

Phoebe's daughter Hope is being brought up a Gottlieb after her mum's marriage to good-natured Stephen Gottlieb, but no one in Ramsay Street will ever forget who Hope's natural father is, as Todd was one of the Street's best-loved neighbours.

NICK PAGE

When Nick's parents died he was only eight years old, so he was taken in by his grandmother who took very good care of him. Even though they never had much money, Nick wanted for little and he was a well balanced kid who loved his granny dearly.

However, as his grandmother got older and frail, their roles reversed and Nick started to take care of his elderly guardian. Nick took a part-time job in a supermarket to help pay for the things they needed, and consequently he started missing a lot of school.

His grandmother became too ill to enforce any discipline on Nick, and so he virtually stopped going to school and went off the rails.

It's at this point in his life that Nick first came to the attention of the neighbours. For a week or so, the Ramsay Street brigade had noticed spray-painted murals in the neighbourhood, and the hunt was on to find the culprit.

It was Henry Ramsay who caught Nick redhanded as he treated Erinsborough to another example of his graffiti art. The neighbours wondered what sort of punishment would be suitable for the wayward sixteen-year-old, and it was Helen Daniels who finally suggested how Nick should be dealt with.

A talented artist herself, Helen recognised real talent in Nick's graffiti and she wanted to encourage him to paint. But that meant leaving his grandma and moving into the Robinson house where Helen could instil young Nick with some discipline. She also hoped to knock off the chip on his shoulder that made him moody and difficult.

In the end it was his grandmother who made Nick make the move, as she realised he stood a greater chance of success with Helen.

Nick clashed badly with Todd who resented the presence of another teenage boy in the house, but Nick was more interested in his art than fighting with Todd. He also had another distraction – his girlfriend Sharon Davies.

Nick and Sharon got into plenty of trouble together as they both had a wild streak a mile wide! But Helen managed to keep him relatively focused on his art, and Nick started to exhibit some of his work.

He applied to study art at a college in London, and the college were so impressed with him that they offered him a scholarship. Nick was over the moon and couldn't wait to leave. He made his goodbyes brief, but reserved special thanks for Helen because if it hadn't been for her he could well have ended up in prison instead of art school.

MELANIE PEARSON

'Mad' Melanie Pearson made her first trip to Erinsborough on the arm of her then boyfriend Henry Ramsay, and returned a year later as Paul Robinson's temp secretary. She was a nightmare to work with, but Paul couldn't pretend she wasn't good at her job and kept her on.

She moved in with Des Clarke at Number 28, and did a grand job of helping to cheer him up following the death of his wife Daphne. In fact Melanie

cheered up everyone's lives with her zany personality, wacky outfits and outrageous laugh – she
sounded like a seal having a hernia!

Melanie became great friends with the Alessi twins
Christina and Caroline, and when Des sold Number
28 to the Willis family, Melanie moved in with the
twins. Melanie was a good friend – if she liked you
she'd do anything for you, but generally she wasn't
asked to do much as she could only be relied upon
to turn everything into a farce! Like the day of
Chrissie's wedding when she turned up to the service
wearing the bride's dress! She caused even more
havoc later that day, when she fell asleep on board
the cruise ship that Paul and Chrissie were honey-
mooning on and ended up staying for the ride!

That wasn't Melanie's first taste of life aboard a
cruise ship. A few years previously she had gone on
a cruise with the express intention of landing herself
a rich husband.

So when she returned to Ramsay Street and
announced she was engaged to Roger, her friends
thought she was making him up so as not to lose
face. Eventually, Roger turned up to sweep Melanie
off her feet, and although Mel was thrilled, her pals
tried to warn her off Roger because he was twice her
age.

But plucky Mel was not to be put off by an age
gap and set about making plans for her own nuptials.
Even the fact that Roger had a fourteen-year-old
daughter wasn't going to dissuade her from the
marriage. It was only when Mel met Tania, Roger's
daughter, that she realised she was taking on too
much.

Tania resented Mel taking her mother's place, and

Melanie wasn't that good at taking care of a moody adolescent and so she broke off her engagement.

Mel was beginning to feel that she would never find love, but she certainly wasn't going to stop looking! She couldn't believe her luck when good looking and charming Simon Hunter, a client of Lassiter's, asked her out on a date.

Before long they were engaged, and everyone congratulated them. But there was one person in Ramsay Street who wasn't pleased that Melanie was finally settling down – her landlord Joe Mangel.

Joe had recently realised that he was in love with Melanie. Ever since his wife Kerry had died, Melanie had been a very good friend to him, helping him raise his children, Toby and Sky. She had even offered to marry him if it would help him win his custody battle for little Sky.

However, Joe knew he had no right to interfere with Melanie's happiness and so he set about finding himself a partner of his own. His quest for love took him to the TV show *Dream Date* in which he was to be a contestant.

Typically, Melanie went along to the studios for moral support, and typically, because of another Melanie mess, she ended up also being one of the contestants! And even though she disguised her voice, Joe still ended up choosing her to be his dream date.

The couple won a romantic weekend for two, and on their first night Joe revealed his true feelings for Melanie, and she realised she felt the same way too!

It was the wedding Ramsay Street had longed for more than any other, and after their happy wedding they left for a new life in Europe taking little Sky with them. Although they never returned, everyone in Ramsay Street wished these two misfits all the happiness in the world.

MATT ROBINSON

Matt was the natural son of Jim's cousin Hilary but was adopted at birth and brought up in Adelaide by Mr and Mrs Williams.

Although he had a good childhood and loved his mum and dad dearly, Matt still wanted to seek out his natural parents and he tracked the stuffy and proper Hilary down to Ramsay Street.

Hilary is not anyone's ideal mother – she barely scrapes through in the wicked stepmother stakes – and Matt was disappointed when she showed no interest in getting to know him. It turned out that Hilary was simply ashamed of the neighbours finding out she'd had an illegitimate child (Matt was the result of a fling when Hilary was twenty).

Eventually Matt forced his mother to reveal his true identity to the rest of the Robinson clan, and mother and son began to form a strong relationship. In fact, Matt became so fond of his formidable mother that he even decided to start using her name, Robinson.

Matt had another reason for staying put in Ramsay Street as he had fallen for his neighbour Sharon Davies. After splitting from his live-in love Lee who had moved to Erinsborough to be with him, Matt found his eye wandering again. But he had a rival for Sharon's affections in the form of Nick Page, and the two lads fought for her.

Although Nick was the eventual victor, Matt soon found a more suitable partner in newcomer Gemma

151

Ramsay. The young couple fell deeply in love and Matt finally felt that Ramsay Street was becoming his home.

There was just one piece in the jigsaw missing – the identity of his natural father. Hilary was cagey about revealing the mystery man's identity, but Matt was soon to come face to face with his dad anyway.

Barry Dwyer checked in as a guest at Lassiter's where Matt was working as a bell boy. Barry had little interest in getting to know his son, but it was enough for Matt to finally put a face to the name.

Matt and Gemma's relationship took a serious turn when they decided to go on holiday together. But a car crash put an unfortunate stop to their vacation plans when Gemma ended up in hospital.

Gemma's dad Tom went to visit her in the hospital, and took every opportunity to attack Matt for being irresponsible and unsuitable for his beloved daughter. He couldn't help wishing that Gemma had never split up with her previous boyfriend Aidan.

Aidan was having similar thoughts himself, and made his way to Ramsay Street to tell Gemma how he really felt. Gemma managed to persuade Matt that Aidan was just a 'good friend'. Nothing happened between Gemma and Aidan, but she couldn't deny that she still had feelings for her ex.

Matt became jealous and in his mind he felt that Gemma was cheating on him, and so he made plans to return to Adelaide. Gemma found him just as he was getting in a taxi to take him away from Ramsay Street, but even though she finally made him believe she hadn't been unfaithful, she couldn't persuade him to stay. If he couldn't trust her, then he couldn't stay with her, he explained, and he tearfully got inside the cab and said goodbye to Erinsborough for good.

MIKE YOUNG

A school friend of Scott Robinson's, Mike seemed a nice well-adjusted young guy with a bright future. But the truth was Mike had known more hardship in his teenage years than his Ramsay Street pal could imagine.

For years, Mike and his mum Barbara had been systematically beaten by his father David. As Mike's important school exam, the HSC, drew closer, he was desperate to leave his family's clutches and give himself a chance of success.

When charitable Daphne Lawrence found out about Mike's situation she helped the young man to make some arrangements with his parents. The plan was to persuade Barbara to leave her husband so that she and Mike could make a new start.

But Barbara was so fearful of her husband's retribution if she left that she couldn't find the courage to make the break.

So Daphne offered Mike the chance to come and live with her and her fiancé Des at Number 28 Ramsay Street. Mike was entitled to some government funding, but he still had to supplement this with regular shifts at Daphne's Coffee Shop.

Mike posed few problems for his neighbours – even his saxophone playing was fairly quiet! He was studious and bright and it was always clear that he would go to university to study to become a teacher.

One of Mike's greatest contributions to *Neighbours* was his introduction of Bouncer as a puppy.

But after carefully tending to Bouncer's every need until he was fully grown, the mutt repaid him by going to live with Mrs Mangel!

Mike was great mates with Scott next door, and Mike often hung out with Scott and his girlfriend Charlene Mitchell.

Sometimes he felt like a bit of a gooseberry, but that all changed when Mrs Mangel's granddaughter Jane Harris moved into Ramsay Street. She took an instant shine to Mike, but because she was a geeky brainbox with goofy glasses she thought Mike would never notice her.

But she was wrong and Mike withstood plenty of jibes from the other lads at school when he started paying her attention. When the school dance came up Mike asked Jane to be his date, although he was unsure about taking such a frump to such a glitzy evening.

But with a little morale and dressmaking help from Daphne and Helen Daniels, Jane was transformed into the confident belle of the ball and it was with pride (and a little disbelief!) that Mike escorted his girlfriend to the dance.

Mike and Jane made quite a foursome with Scott and Charlene, and the teenagers spent most of their time in each other's company. The apple-cart was nearly upset by the arrival of Helen Daniels' niece Nikki Dennison who did her conniving best to split Mike and Jane up.

Tough times were afoot for Mike. News came to Erinsborough that his abusive father had died. Although there was no love lost between father and son, it was still an emotional time.

While there was no doubting that Mike and Jane were good for each other, they were never as madly in love as Scott and Charlene, and they graciously accepted their supporting roles of best man and bridesmaid at their pals' wedding.

They stole a little of the limelight for themselves when Mike's photo (he was a keen amateur photographer) of Jane was selected as the poster for the first Lassiter's girl.

However, Mike and Jane were not destined to stay together. They split up amicably and agreed to stay friends. Jane went off on her international modelling career, but Mike stayed true to his dream of qualifying as a teacher at university.

During his first stint of teacher training where he was put on placement at Erinsborough High, Mike landed himself in hot water when the principal caught him kissing one of his pupils in an empty classroom.

In a bid to save his career, Mike left Erinsborough for somewhere where his teaching reputation was untarnished. He later returned to Ramsay Street where he was dismayed to find Jane had fallen head over heels in love with his mate Des. He still hoped for a reconciliation with Jane, so when she got engaged to Des he consoled himself with a futile one night stand. He left Erinsborough shortly afterwards, keen not to let Jane see how he really felt.

RAMSAY STREET AND ERINSBOROUGH

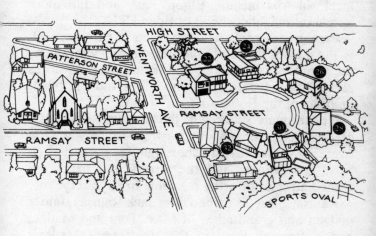

Every city in the world has a suburb like Erinsborough – and that's part of the appeal of *Neighbours*. Erinsborough is populated, on the whole, by people with a bit of spare money in their pockets to spend on the nice things in life.

Some houses, like Number 24 Ramsay Street, have swimming pools, and almost all have gardens. All of the houses are in a good state of repair and nicely decorated. Basically, Erinsborough is a very pleasant place.

It's a safe area to bring up a family and a convenient place – Erinsborough High School is within walking distance and in the neighbouring suburb of Anson's Corner there is a big shopping centre. Other local suburbs include Elliott Park and the more upmarket neighbourhood of Eden Hills.

Perhaps one of the greatest assets of Erinsborough is the Lassiter's hotel complex which incorporates the popular Coffee Shop, The Waterhole pub, stores as well as first-rate accommodation and the headquarters of the Robinson Corporation.

Unlike many suburbs in the relatively new cities of Australia (remember, Australia is only a little over 200 years old) Erinsborough has roots that go back generations, and the streets and parks are named after noteworthy residents from yesteryear.

Ramsay Street is named after Jack Ramsay, father of Dan and grandfather of Max, Tom and Madge, and a Ramsay lived in the street until Madge's departure in 1993.

Although the cul-de-sac which is seen on screen only has six houses, the numbers of those houses go from 22 to 32. This is because the Ramsay Street we see is in fact just the end of a long road, and the rest of the Ramsay Street house numbers are on the other side of the main road which bisects it (see map).

Life in the street is generally quiet, with only the sounds of lawnmowers, and dogs barking to interrupt the suburban bliss.

The only time Ramsay Street's future was ever really in doubt was in 1988 when Paul Robinson attempted to buy the land for a supermarket development. His family and his friends were disgusted that he would try to buy their homes from them in such a callous manner, and in the end they stalled the deal so badly that the developer gave up the plans.

NUMBER 22

The first featured resident of Number 22 was Clive
Gibbons who upset the neighbours, notably Mrs
Mangel of course, with his brightly painted station-
wagon called Bertha. The neighbours were also
slightly dubious about Clive's choice of profession
when it was discovered that he ran a gorilla-gram
service.

It was only when Clive performed a life-saving
tracheotomy on Lucy on the Robinsons' kitchen
table that it was revealed that he was in fact a doctor
who had turned his back on medicine.

Clive was the joker of Ramsay Street in those days
and many people overlooked him, dismissing him
simply as a clown. But the truth was Clive was a
very loving man and he took in Susan Cole and baby
Sam when they had nowhere else to go. Naturally
he was wonderful with children and he fell for the
little boy. His affection for Susan developed soon
afterwards although Clive was too much of a gentleman to make a pass at her.

He was good mates with Shane Ramsay and
together they started RAGGS (Ramsay and Gibbons Gardening Services) while still managing to run
his Gift of the Gab communications service on the
side.

During his time at Number 22, Clive also offered

a roof and a room (like all Ramsay Street houses, Number 22 has a varying number of bedrooms according to the storyline!) to Daphne, Zoe and Mike Young.

It was only when Paul started to implement his plan to buy Ramsay Street in order to clear the way to build an access road to a planned supermarket in 1988, that Clive was given notice to quit the house. However, when the deal was scrapped, Clive stuck around for a few more months.

When Clive left, Paul – who now owned the house – decided to live in it himself. The first person to join him there was his second wife (by arranged marriage) Gail Lewis. Although the couple eventually fell in love and retook their marriage vows, their union did not last long because Paul always put work before his wife.

After Gail left him, Paul moved into a suite at Lassiter's and rented the house to Caroline and Christina Alessi, who collectively used the name Linda Giles when one of them signed the lease. However, it wasn't long before Paul returned to Number 22 as the twins soon asked Paul to be their lodger! As a wedding present to Chrissie, Paul put the deeds of the house in her name and the three of them lived happily at Number 22 until Paul and Caroline's affair in 1993.

The fall-out from their affair caused all three to leave Erinsborough and the house was then occupied by the twins' aunt and uncle Cathy and Benito Alessi, and their two sons Marco and Rick.

In April 1994, Benito took up a new post in Sydney, leaving Number 22 vacant. For a time it was rented to the Lim family before Cheryl Starke and her brood moved in.

NUMBER 24

This house was in the hands of the Ramsay family from the day it was built until 1993, when Madge finally left Erinsborough for a new life in Brisbane.

In the early days of *Neighbours* it was owned and occupied by local plumber Max Ramsay. When he left for Brisbane in an attempt to repair his marriage to Maria in 1987, he left the house in the hands of his brother Tom who bought the house with the help of his sister Madge who lent him most of the money on the grounds that he pay her back.

When Madge followed her brothers to Ramsay Street, they talked about selling the house as Madge needed to get her hands on the money. When the siblings did their calculations they worked out that Tom had repaid enough money to make them equal partners, 50:50. It was a stalemate and so they both agreed to stay.

However, Tom left in 1988 to live with his daughter Moira, and Madge had severe difficulties in meeting the mortgage. It was only Shane's rent that kept her financially afloat. But her new job at The Waterhole eased the strain on Madge's budget so that when Shane shot through she could afford to stay put.

The deeds to the house stayed in Madge's name while Charlene, Henry, Scott, Bronwyn and Sharon stayed. After her marriage to Harold Bishop, Madge had another lodger, Tom's younger daughter, Gemma.

In 1992, after a win on the Premium Bonds, Madge and Harold decided to celebrate their luck by taking extended leave from their day-to-day lives and touring Australia. In their absence, they rented the house to Brenda Riley, the younger sister of Madge's old flame Lou Carpenter.

Brenda shared the house with her nephew Guy before Madge's sad return following Harold's disappearance. On her return, Madge came face to face with ex-lover Lou, but their half-hearted romance couldn't help her forget Harold, and the couple agreed to split.

While Madge went to join the rest of the Ramsays in Brisbane, Lou took on the responsibility of Number 24. He embarked on a silly affair with seventeen-year-old Annalise Hartman, who was later to become one of his many lodgers.

In a bid to make himself feel younger, Lou opened up his house to a string of teenagers including his sensible daughter Lauren. Other tenants included Cameron Hudson, Beth Brennan, Brad Willis for a while and also Rick Alessi who became like a son to Lou.

The young, firm bodies of the assorted lodgers made plenty of use of the swimming pool in the garden, as it was only one of two houses in Ramsay Street to have such a facility (the other is Number 30).

NUMBER 26

Until Jim's death in early 1994, Number 26 Ramsay Street had been known as the Robinson house. Ever since *Neighbours* began, Jim ruled the roost at Number 26, aided and abetted by his trusty mother-in-law Helen Daniels.

Their charges at the time were Jim's children Paul, Julie, Scott and Lucy. Julie was the first to leave the nest when, in 1987, she went to care for her lover Philip Martin and his two children.

Paul was the next to go, moving out of the room he shared with his brother to a suite at Lassiter's (he later returned to Ramsay Street and moved into Number 22).

Lucy and Scott didn't hang around either: Lucy gladly packed her bags and went off to boarding school (although Jim kept her room free for home visits) and Scott moved next door when he married Charlene Mitchell.

But Number 26 was not to be free from teenagers. When Jim married Beverly Marshall, the newlyweds became legal guardians of Todd and Katie Landers, Beverly's nephew and niece. Katie returned to live with her mother Annette in Adelaide after a couple of years, but Todd remained in Erinsborough where he was at a crucial point in his school career.

When the parents of Todd's friend Josh Anderson

moved away from the neighbourhood, Jim and Helen agreed to take Josh in as a lodger. They also took in aspiring artist Nick Page when Helen feared that his talent might go to waste, adding to the long list of Ramsay Street orphans.

Lucy soon returned from boarding school, and her long lost brother Glen Donnelly turned up on the doorstep of Number 26, and yet again the Robinson house was bustling. But that's just the way Helen and Jim liked it.

In 1993, Lucy left Erinsborough and Australia for a new modelling career in Singapore, and Glen left as quickly as he had come after being paralysed in a construction site accident. That meant the house was empty for the reappearance of Julie and her family who returned to Erinsborough for Todd's funeral.

Julie's husband Philip Martin had lost his job and the family could no longer afford to live where they were. So Helen and Jim insisted they stay with them until they were back on their feet.

Julie and Philip had a child of their own, Hannah, and they also looked after Philip's kids from his first marriage, Debbie and Michael.

When Jim announced that he had been having an affair with the man-eater Fiona Hartman in early 1994, Helen and Julie were so upset by the news (and as they hated Fiona so vehemently) they both moved across the road to Number 32, a house Helen had bought the previous year as an investment.

Shortly after their swift departure, Jim collapsed and died of a heart attack in the kitchen at Number 26. Fiona tried to take control of the house, but was hounded out of town by her enemies. A sad Helen returned to live at Number 26 with only lodger Wayne Duncan for company.

Helen rattled around in the big house without her family there, but she said she could never be lonely at Number 26 because the house was filled with so many happy memories.

NUMBER 28

Assistant bank manager Des Clarke bought Number 28 with a specially arranged mortgage as a family home for himself and his bride-to-be Lorraine Kingham. However, when Lorraine jilted him on the morning of their wedding in 1986, Des found himself in desperate need of a lodger to help him keep up the mortgage repayments.

The woman who offered to pay him rent was the stripper from his buck's night, Daphne Lawrence. It took Des and Daphne a long time to admit how they really felt about each other, but finally – at the second attempt – the two of them married.

Daphne had already become legal guardian to Erinsborough High pupil Mike Young who moved in with the couple. Mike's own addition to the family was a cute labrador puppy called Bouncer who was to become one of Ramsay Street's regulars.

Des and Daphne also made an addition of their own to the household when they produced their first son, Jamie. Sadly, Jamie would grow up never knowing his mother as Daphne was killed in a car crash in 1989.

Mike left Erinsborough soon afterwards and Des and Jamie were left on their own apart from the intermittent presence of Des's interfering mother Eileen.

Des was in desperate need of a live-in nanny as he tried to rebuild his career after Daphne's death. The job – and a room – went to country girl Bronwyn Davies.

Bronwyn also lived with Mrs Mangel at Number 32 before moving to the Ramsay House to share with her boyfriend Henry Ramsay, and Des realised that there was nothing really left for him and Jamie in Erinsborough. He went to Perth to be with his mother and search for work. When he landed a stockbroker's job (and a girlfriend), Des returned to Ramsay Street to put Number 28 on the market.

He sold to the parents of Todd Landers' girlfriend Cody Willis, Pam and Doug.

Pam worked as a nurse at the local hospital and Doug owned his own construction company and it looked like they would have no problems coping with the expenses of living in Ramsay Street. But unbeknown to their children Cody and Adam – their other kids Gaby and Brad were studying abroad – Pam and Doug were having severe financial problems and at one point it looked like they would have to sell up and move out.

However, when Gaby returned from her course in Japan she fooled a client of Doug's who owed a lot of money that she was the family lawyer and got him to pay up. It was the turning point for the Willises, who gradually turned their fortunes around.

Brad soon followed his sister to Ramsay Street after playing basketball in America. As Adam had left to study in Newcastle and Cody had left for a student exchange in the States, it meant there was no shortage of beds!

NUMBER 30

Unlike the previous houses, Number 30 hasn't always been occupied by characters throughout the run of *Neighbours*. Intermittently when the storyline had required the use of another house viewers have occasionally been taken behind the front door.

The first known occupants of this house were Paul and his first wife Terri Inglis, who moved in after Jim rented them the property as a wedding present.

It was in the front room of this house that Terri shot Paul in the shoulder and left him to die. Terri was jailed for her crime and understandably Paul had no wish to stay in the house after the shooting and he returned temporarily to his father's house at Number 26.

Between 1987 and 1991 the house was occupied by people who were never seen on screen. The next featured resident was Erinsborough High School principal Dorothy Burke who quickly took in her niece and nephew, 'Lochy' and Ryan McLachlan.

Lochy returned to her mother and Ryan left to join the army, but prickly Dorothy didn't let her spare rooms stand empty for long. Her first 'acquisition' was Toby Mangel (who of course brought Bouncer with him) who stayed with Mim – as he called her – after his dad Joe and stepmum Melanie left for England.

Dorothy's other charge was also a pupil of hers, Phoebe Bright. Phoebe was one of her most talented and brightest students, and Dorothy was determined that Phoebe have the best opportunity to complete her HSC after the unexpected death of her father.

But what Dorothy didn't bank on was Phoebe falling in love – and falling pregnant! After losing her virginity to Todd Landers, Phoebe discovered she was expecting. Her immediate decision was to have an abortion, and Dorothy took on the role of surrogate mother and took Phoebe to the clinic for her operation. But at the last minute, they learnt that Todd had been in an accident and Phoebe decided not to go through with the termination.

Dorothy and Phoebe rushed to Todd's bedside only to watch him die. With Todd gone, there was no way Phoebe was going to give up the baby, and she gave up her education instead.

By chance, at Todd's graveside, Phoebe bumped into a caring young man called Stephen Gottlieb who had also lost his partner. He proposed to Phoebe within weeks and they were married in 1993.

Love was also round the corner for Dorothy who, after her disastrous marriage to her fraudulent husband Colin, thought she would never find love again. But Education Inspector Tom Merrick swept her off her feet and took her – and Toby – off to a new life in the country.

That left the house to Stephen, Phoebe and their baby daughter Hope.

In order to meet the expenses of living at Number 30 they were forced to take in a lodger. When Russell Butler answered their ad in early 1994, they thought they'd found the perfect tenant.

But Russell was in fact deranged after his girlfriend had left him with their baby – and Russell thought Phoebe and Hope would make perfect replacements. It took several months for Russell's true colours to show, but during that time Phoebe and Stephen were unnerved and tiptoed on eggshells in their own home.

Things finally came to a head when Russell snatched Hope from Phoebe while she was hanging out the washing, and Stephen knew he had to do something about it. He arranged for a gang of thugs to give Russell a fright, but they lynched Wayne Duncan instead, in a case of mistaken identity. However, the message eventually got through to Russell and he was made to leave town.

This still left Phoebe and Russell with money worries, but the solution came when Beth Brennan became their next, and less troublesome, lodger.

NUMBER 32

When *Neighbours* started the incumbents at Number 32 were Len and Nell Mangel, although Len was never seen.

The sensible man soon deserted his bickering, nagging and abominable wife, leaving Mrs Mangel no choice but to terrorise her neighbours instead!

In 1987, Nell's studious granddaughter Jane Harris was sent to live with her, but the two women were soon joined by Bouncer the dog! Bouncer could obviously tell that Nell was a lonely old woman, and he did his bit for the community by taking care of her.

Nell remarried late in life and her son Joe arrived in Erinsborough for the wedding. He had obviously rebelled against his prim and proper mother and had turned into something of a slob. Still, he was a gardener by trade and soon the garden at Number 32 looked like the Melbourne Botanical Gardens – Joe even had a bet with Harold Bishop once to see who could win a competition for Erinsborough's finest garden!

For a time Jane and Joe shared the house, but it was inevitable that their tastes and lifestyles would clash. Jane found things even harder going when Joe's ex-wife Noeline dumped their eight-year-old son Toby at Number 32.

Jane left shortly afterwards to be with her grandmother in England, and before long Joe and Toby had been joined by Kerry and Sky Bishop, after a whirlwind romance and wedding for Kerry and Joe.

Kerry was killed in a shooting accident by poachers in 1991 and Joe found himself in need of help with the kids. Luckily Toby and Sky got on brilliantly with their lodger, mad Melanie Pearson. Unexpectedly, Joe also got on extremely well with Mel and they fell in love and married.

When they left for their honeymoon in Europe in 1992, they took Sky with them and Toby went to live next door with Dorothy Burke.

The house was put on the market and sold through auction. The woman who put in the highest bid on the day was Rosemary Daniels, but she later revealed that she had been buying on behalf of her mum Helen who wanted the house as an investment.

The house was rented at one time to Faye Hudson and her son Cameron who had both left Erinsborough by the time Helen's granddaughter Julie and her family needed the house.

They rented from Helen – Helen even lived with them herself for a short time because she was fighting with Jim's girlfriend Fiona Hartman so badly – on the understanding that they would buy it as soon as they were able.

There was enough room for all the kids, Debbie, Hannah and Michael if he wants to come home, as well as the latest addition to the family, Holly the dog.

THE NEIGHBOURS
FACT FILE

ON SCREEN!

A quick glance at the Erinsborough registrar's files show that you shouldn't move to the neighbourhood if you want to get pregnant! Astoundingly, in *Neighbours*' long history only three babies have been born to the residents of Ramsay Street.

You should also stay away from the area if you fancy living a long life, as the neighbourhood has a particularly high death rate.

On the upside though, Erinsborough is a mecca for weddings! Since the show started, fourteen couples have made it to the altar to say 'I do'. Four other couples (Des and Daphne, Eileen and Malcolm, Glen and Karen and Beth and Brad) have had the weddings organised, but the services have turned into shambles before the vows were exchanged.

Three of the weddings were Paul's, making him the most married neighbour, and two of them were Joe Mangel's.

BIRTHS

James Kingsley Clarke   December 1988

Daphne Clarke unexpectedly went into labour on the 6th while enjoying a picnic with her husband

Des. Thankfully doctor Beverly arrived just in time to deliver baby Jamie.

Andrew Robinson   November 1992

Chrissie was on her way to the shops when she suddenly went into labour on the 10th. Thankfully her twin sister Caroline started to have sympathetic labour pains, and alerted dad Paul to get Chrissie to the maternity ward in time.

Hope Gottlieb   November 1993

Little Hope arrived two months prematurely – the day before her mum Phoebe was due to marry Stephen Gottlieb. Her birth postponed the wedding for a couple of weeks.

DEATHS

Jean Richardson   December 1987

After the reception for Des and Daphne's wedding, Shane Ramsay took Jean, his uncle Tom's girlfriend, to the airport. But his car tyre suffered a blow out and he crashed the car killing Jean instantly.

Terri Inglis Robinson   April 1988

While Paul tried to start a new relationship with his secretary Susan Cole, he received news that his first wife Terri had committed suicide in prison.

Jeremy Lord   October 1988

Gail Robinson's first husband Jeremy knew he was dicing with death when he took to the racing track in a notorious classic racing car called Number Thirteen. Rob, Jim and Gail were all present when the car went into an uncontrollable spin, which killed Jeremy instantly.

Daphne Lawrence/Clarke   July 1989

Daphne had been in a coma for two months after being in a car crash. Her husband Des always believed she would come out of her coma, but she only woke briefly to say 'I love you Clarkey' before finally slipping away on the 3rd.

Noeline Mangel   July 1991

The death of his mother sent young Toby into a depression, but he was helped by his stepmum Kerry who he soon learned to call 'mum' in Noeline's place.

Kerry Bishop   October 1991

Joe had tried to discourage his environmentally aware wife from going on a protest to stop game poaching. He always wished he had tried harder after she was killed by a poacher's stray bullet on the 22nd.

Harold Bishop   October 1992

While on holiday with his wife Madge, Harold took a walk along the cliffs. One minute he was there, the next he was missing, presumed drowned, although his body was never recovered.

Garth Kirby   February 1993

An old friend of Pam and Doug, Garth was an elderly craftsman who was dying of cancer. He was in unbearable pain and asked both Pam and Doug to administer an overdose. Both refused, but when Garth finally passed away, Pam was still arrested for his murder. She was later acquitted.

Todd Landers   June 1993

Todd was in such a rush to get to the clinic to stop his girlfriend Phoebe Bright from having an abortion that he didn't see a van as he tried to cross a busy road. He was knocked down and taken to hospital where he suffered a massive heart attack and died.

Jim Robinson   March 1994

Jim had had several minor heart scares before, but he hoped a fitness regime would mean he wouldn't be affected any more. But after a strenuous play session with his granddaughter Hannah, Jim returned to Number 26 for a lie-down. However, he suffered a massive heart attack and died.

MARRIAGES

Terri Inglis and Paul Robinson   April 1987

Paul proposed to Terri after just one date. The marriage proved to be almost as short-lived as the courtship, when Terri shot Paul and left him for dead a few months later.

Andrea Townsend and Jack Lassiter
December 1987

Des's ex-girlfriend Andrea made older man Jack very happy when she agreed to marry him. The couple later emigrated with Andrea's son Bradley.

Daphne Lawrence and Des Clarke   December 1987

It was second time lucky for this pair. They failed at the first attempt in July when Des thought Daphne wasn't coming. In fact, she had been held hostage by an armed bank robber!

Edna Ramsay and Dan Ramsay   March 1988

Edna thought she had already been married to Dan for fifty years, but when she filed for divorce after Dan's philanderings she discovered her marriage had never been legal! Dan had been so incompetent he'd never filed the marriage certificate. Eventually, Edna agreed to give him a second chance and they made it legal on the 1st.

Gail Lewis and Paul Robinson   October 1988

Work colleagues Gail and Paul only married to gain a business contract from traditional Japanese businessman Mr Udugawa. They invited their relatives round for dinner to Number 22, and surprised them with an impromptu ceremony on the 25th.

Charlene Mitchell and Scott Robinson
November 1988

The soap wedding of the century! Teenagers Scott and Charlene tied the knot in a traditional and emotional church service on the 8th. Mike was best man, Jane and Lucy were bridesmaids and Henry gave his little sister away.

Beverly Marshall and Jim Robinson   May 1989

Screened in Australia on Valentine's Day, Bev and Jim beat Madge and Harold to first rights to wed on this romantic day. Paul and Gail also got in on the act when they renewed their vows at the service.

Madge Ramsay and Harold Bishop   August 1989

Madge and Harold finally tied the knot on the 18th when Reverend Sampson pronounced them man and wife.

Nell Mangel and John Worthington   February 1990

Everyone in Erinsborough breathed a sigh of relief on the 1st, as they knew John was taking the shrewish Nell away with him to England the following day!

Kerry Bishop and Joe Mangel   April 1990

After a courtship of several months, single parents Kerry and Joe said 'I do' in the romantic setting of a butterfly house.

Bouncer and Rosie   August 1991

OK, so it was only in his dream that Bouncer woofed 'I do' to his favourite sheepdog Rosie, but everyone knows that Bouncer was really human!

Christina Alessi and Paul Robinson   February 1992

Her wedding on the 19th was the day Chrissie had waited for since the day she had first laid eyes on Paul. She fought off her sister and the scheming Isabella Lopez to get Paul down the aisle.

Helen Daniels and Michael Daniels   July 1992

This was Helen's second marriage – her first had been to Michael's cousin Bill. Sadly, it was also Michael's second marriage, but he was still married to his first wife and his marriage to Helen was later annulled.

Phoebe Bright and Stephen Gottlieb   November 1993

Stephen had originally intended to wed Phoebe at the beginning of the month, but the premature arrival of their daughter Hope meant that they had to postpone their wedding plans. Their big day was generally a happy affair, marred only by the unwanted arrival of Stephen's musician parents.

OFF SCREEN!

REAL LIFE ROMANCE

The romantic shenanigans of the *Neighbours* cast have more than kept up with those of their on-screen counterparts. In fact the *Neighbours* studio has been a veritable hotbed of romance! Here's a list of couples who met through the programme.

Vikki Blanche and David Clencie

Although David was quite a bit younger than Vikki, the couple still lived together for a while.

Anne Haddy and James Condon

Anne and James didn't actually meet on the set. By the time James played bad guy Douglas Blake, he had been married to Anne for several years!

Elaine Smith and Peter O'Brien

For a time these two played lovers on screen, and friends expected them to marry in real life. However, they split after four years and Peter married British actress Jo Riding.

Kylie Minogue and Jason Donovan

Every newspaper in Australia speculated that their on-screen romance was mirrored in real life. Although the couple denied it, co-star Stefan Dennis confirmed the romance in an interview with a British magazine. Kylie and Jason both later admitted that they had dated for about four years.

Fiona Corke and Nick Caraffa

Nick made a guest appearance in the show as Coffee Shop helper Tony Romeo, but he made a more lasting impression on Fiona and they are still together, although they haven't married.

Rachel Friend and Craig McLachlan

Craig was already married when he joined the *Neighbours* cast, but when he divorced his wife Karen, he started dating Rachel, imitating the on-screen affair between their characters Bronwyn and Henry. After a long engagement, Craig and Rachel married in early 1993.

Gayle Blakeney and Stefan Dennis

These lovebirds sadly split up after more than two years together, and Stefan later admitted that Gayle had been the love of his life. Their romance followed the on-screen pairing, and eventual marriage, of their characters Chrissie and Paul.

Simone Robertson and Benjamin Mitchell

Simone was only seventeen when she fell for 24-

year-old Ben. Despite the age gap, the couple stayed together and exchanged silver rings. They share a house in Melbourne.

Kimberley Davies and Scott Michaelson

Kim and Scott had dated before Kim started her role as Annalise, but their romance was over before she joined the cast. However, rumours that they had got back together abounded for a long time.

QUICK CHANGE!

Neighbours is famous for recasting characters with different actors, and it's no surprise! Just look at this list of characters that suddenly appeared looking very different!

Character	Actor
Scott Robinson	1. Darius Perkins 2. Jason Donovan
Lucy Robinson	1. Kylie Flinker 2. Sasha Close 3. Melissa Bell
Julie Robinson Martin	1. Vikki Blanche 2. Julie Mullins
Beverly Robinson	1. Lisa Armytage 2. Shaunna O'Grady

Philip Martin	1. Christopher Milne
	2. Ian Rawlings
Debbie Martin	1. Mandy Storvik
	2. Marnie Reece-Wilmore
Toby Mangel	1. Finn Keane
	2. Ben Geurens
Jamie Clarke	1. S. J. Dey
	2. Ryder Susman
	3. Nicholas Mason
Bob Landers	1. Robin Harrison
	2. Bruce Kilpatrick

FAMOUS FACES

A role in *Neighbours* is a surefire way to fame, even if it's just a small part. Some of the following actors used *Neighbours* as a launch pad to success, and some were famous before they ever set foot in Ramsay Street . . .

Gwen Plumb

A favourite from her days as *The Young Doctors'* lovable gossip Ada, Gwen appeared briefly in *Neighbours* in 1986 as farmer's wife Mrs Forbes.

Deborra Lee-Furness

Deborra was a little known actress when she turned up as bank teller Linda Fielding in 1987. She has since become one of Australia's leading film actresses, winning awards for her work in films like *Shame*.

Nadine Garner

A familiar face on Aussie TV for years before she turned up as a runaway called Rachel in 1987, Nadine had already appeared in the *Henderson Kids* and the film *Mullaway* with Sue Jones. Nadine made her name in Britain with shows like *The Boys From The Bush* and *A Class Act*.

Carole Skinner

A picture of Carole still sits on Helen Daniels' sideboard as she played Helen's late sister Laura Dennison. However, she is better remembered by *Prisoner* fans as baddie Nola McKensie.

Alan Hopgood

By the time Alan appeared in *Neighbours* in 1987 as Jack Lassiter (the original owner of the hotel), he was already well-known as kind-hearted Wally from his days in the soap *Prisoner*.

Warwick Capper

Football hero Warwick played himself in *Neighbours* in early 1988 when he turned up in the Coffee Shop to have a drink with his 'old friend' Des Clarke.

Molly Meldrum

Aussie TV host Molly (a man) also played himself in 1988 when he spotted Charlene and Jane in a talent contest.

Alex Papps

He later made his name as Frank Morgan in *Home and Away*, and then as Nick in *The Flying Doctors*, but he was earlier seen in *Neighbours* in 1988 as Nick Davies who blew up Charlene's caravan.

Russell Crowe

Russell is now one of Australia's leading film actors and has even made a Hollywood film with Sharon Stone. But one of his earlier roles was as Kenny Larkin in *Neighbours* in 1989.

Mat Stevenson

Mat found international fame in rival soap *Home and Away* as Adam Cameron. But for several months in 1990 he played baddie Skinner who tried to lead Todd off the straight and narrow.

Abigail

Considered a sex siren in Australia after she was the first actress to appear nude on Aussie TV (in the soap *Number 96*), Abigail appeared briefly in Ramsay Street in June 1990 as another temptress. She later appeared in the adult soap *Chances*.

Derek Nimmo

This respected English actor appeared as Lord Legerwood, the noble friend of Rosemary when Madge and Harold visited England in 1991.

Brian Blain

When Brian turned up as bearded Michael Daniels, Helen's husband-to-be in 1992, many fans recognised him as *Sons and Daughters*' Gordon Hamilton.

SOAP SWAP!

All these famous *Neighbours* once appeared in starring roles in other soaps from Down Under . . .

Elspeth Ballantyne

Elspeth was a firm favourite after playing *Prisoner*'s Meg Morris for six years before she became Ramsay Street's Cathy Alessi.

Joy Chambers

Before landing the recurring role of Rosemary Daniels, Joy had already made an impression on soap fans as *The Young Doctors'* Dr Robyn Porter.

Alan Dale

Unforgettable as Jim Robinson, but equally memorable as *The Young Doctors'* Dr Forrest.

Maggie Dence

Before she starred in *Neighbours* as the formidable Dorothy Burke, she cut her soap teeth playing *Prisoner*'s Bev Baker.

Ally Fowler

Fans of *Sons and Daughters* couldn't believe their eyes when Ally turned up in Ramsay Street as Zoe Davis – she was much more familiar to them as Angela Hamilton.

Vivean Gray

Vivean played *Neighbours'* supreme gossip Mrs Mangel, but she also played the best gossip with the sharpest tongue in *The Sullivans* – Mrs Jessop.

Anne Haddy

Before becoming everybody's favourite granny as Helen Daniels, Anne was everybody's favourite house-keeper as Rosie Andrews in *Sons and Daughters*.

Richard Huggett

Before playing mild-mannered Glen Donnelly, Richard made an impression on soap fans as psychotic Sonny Bennet in *E Street*.

Maxine Kliblingaitis

In *Neighbours* her character Terri ended up in prison – maybe it was Wentworth Detention Centre, the 'home' of her *Prisoner* character Bobbie Mitchell.

Craig McLachlan

Craig went straight from Ramsay Street to Summer Bay, swapping Henry Ramsay for *Home and Away*'s schoolteacher Grant Mitchell.

Richard Norton

Richard also made the crossover to Summer Bay, taking on the role of Simon Fitzgerald after leaving behind *Neighbours'* Ryan McLachlan.

Peter O'Brien

After leaving Shane Ramsay behind him, Peter went on to star in *The Flying Doctors* as Sam Patterson.

Ashley Paske

Ashley starred in the short-lived soap *Richmond Hill* as tearaway Marty, before achieving fame as *Neighbours'* Matt Robinson.

Ian Rawlings

He may play a nice guy now as Philip Martin, but for some viewers, Ian will always be remembered as *Sons and Daughters'* evil Wayne Hamilton.

Bruce Samazan

Bruce won several awards, including the Silver Logie, for his portrayal as *E Street*'s constable Max Simmons before he moved to Ramsay Street in the guise of Mark Gottlieb.

CHART SUCCESS

Kylie and Jason aren't the only *Neighbours* stars to have made the crossover into music. All these other

Neighbours have tried their luck – with varying degrees of success!

Albie Wilde and the Dayglos (featuring Fiona Corke, Annie Jones and Guy Pearce) – released a single in Oz called 'Hey Ciao'. Guy also worked on some solo material and sang in a couple of his films.

Felice Arena – under the name 'Moses' he released a club hit in the UK, a cover of the Bee Gees' classic 'More Than a Woman'.

The Blakeney Twins – they made an album for Mushroom records in the UK after chart disappointment 'Down Under'. Their first UK single 'Mad If Ya Don't' flopped, as did the follow up, a cover of the Prince classic 'I Wanna Be Your Lover'.

Anne Charleston and Ian Smith – they released a spoof Christmas record as Madge and Harold.

Stefan Dennis – released two singles in the UK. The first, 'Don't It Make You Feel Good', reached Number 16.

Paul Keane – Paul is a drummer in an Australian pub band.

Craig McLachlan – reached Number 2 in the UK with 'Hey Mona' with his band The Check 1–2. His album was also a chart success.

Ben Mitchell – Ben is a guitarist and vocalist with the pub band Tin Canal.

Bruce Samazan – he released a rap single in Oz called 'One of a Kind' which sadly failed to make an impression.

George Spartels – George regularly sang on TV as the host of *Playskool*. He released a collection of children's songs.

Mark Stevens – a gifted singer, Mark hoped to emulate his idol John Farnham, but negotiations with his record company broke down before his record was released.

Andrew Williams – Andrew had a record contract lined up with Westside, the producers of *E Street*, before the company folded in 1992.

CALENDAR OF EVENTS

(NB These dates refer to UK broadcasts)

1986

October

Des Clarke is jilted on the morning of his wedding on the 27th, *Neighbours'* first day of broadcast in the UK. Danny Ramsay is having unexplainable night-mares. His big brother Shane starts flirting with new resident, stripper Daphne Lawrence.

November

Scott is having girl trouble with Kim Taylor at school. Des worries about what the neighbours will think of him living with Daphne the stripper. Shane is in a car accident which puts paid to his diving career. Maria's sister Anna Rossi begins an affair with Jim Robinson. Eileen Clarke is seen for the first time – and naturally she disapproves of Daphne.

December

Julie Robinson begins to think that there might be a second chance for her and Des. Maria reveals that

195

Danny is not Max's son, but this news is kept from Danny. Scott and Danny leave Erinsborough after altercations with their 'olds' and find work on a farm run by Mrs Forbes. Des is offered a promotion – but it involves a move to Canberra. Max moves out of Number 24 into a bedsit.

1987

January

Plumber Max hires a new assistant over the phone called Terry, but when the new help arrives, he is shocked to see it is a Terri. Belligerent Max is determined to give his female assistant a hard time, but she proves she's as good as any man. She also starts to date Shane.

February

A new manager, Philip Martin, is installed at the Pacific Bank and Julie is drawn to him. Terri reveals her criminal past to Shane and hints that her life may be in danger. Max and Maria try to patch things up, but their romantic dinner turns acrimonious. Jim is concerned about Julie's relationship with Philip, who is married with kids. Shane moves in with his dad.

March

Danny and Scott fight over a girl at school, Wendy Gibson. Philip's wife Loretta threatens Julie with a knife and Philip realises he must leave Julie alone to stop Loretta from killing her. Loretta is revealed to be a drunk. After splitting from Shane, Terri goes out on a date with Paul. At the end of the evening, Paul proposes marriage – and Terri accepts. Maria starts dating Richard Morrison.

April

Danny becomes increasingly more resentful of Richard and in the end gives his mum an ultimatum. Tearfully, Maria decides to leave Ramsay Street to be with Richard. On the 29th, Paul and Terri marry. As a wedding present, Jim rents them Number 30.

May

Max moves back into the Ramsay house. Mysterious art collector Douglas Blake takes an interest in Helen Daniels' paintings. Jim's mum Bess, a respected stateswoman, arrives. She is writing her memoirs which Scott cheekily reads. He is shocked to discover she is dying. Bess swears him to secrecy. Julie is told that Philip has been injured in a car crash which killed Loretta, and she visits him in hospital. Danny takes a job at the bank.

June

Terri's past catches up with her and she is threatened by Charles Durham who is after a mysterious tape which Lucy Robinson has accidentally lost. Julie leaves to take care of the crippled Philip and his kids. While Paul, who has quit university, is away on a flight as an air steward, Shane stays over at Number 30 to protect a scared Terri. The next day, Daphne is nearly run over when she is mistaken for

Terri as she has borrowed her friend's coat. It is clear that Terri is in serious danger. Terri shoots dead Charles Durham. Daphne later discovers his body during a frantic search for Terri. She gets some blood on her skirt and this is enough to have her arrested for his murder. Paul later twigs that Terri has done the deed, and as he phones the police to report her she shoots him in the shoulder and leaves him for dead. Jim later discovers him and he is rushed to hospital. Daphne's grandfather Harry Henderson arrives, and wins the Coffee Shop and gives the shop to Daphne as a present. Helen discovers that Douglas Blake is a con-man who has taken her heart and her money. Danny learns the truth about Max and goes to be with his mother in Brisbane. On the 30th, the new Channel Ten episodes air for the first time bringing several new characters – Clive, Zoe, Mike and Madge.

July

The neighbours gossip about the 'apes' at Number 22 and are not relieved when they meet the real Gibbon, Clive. Helen's niece Nikki Dennison comes to stay at Number 26. Helen wants revenge on Douglas Blake and enlists Madge's help. Jim learns that Scott is expected home a week early from a school trip and suspects something is wrong. It turns out that Scott had been accused of rape and has subsequently run away to avoid arrest. He has disappeared in the bush. Shane and Clive start RAGGS (Ramsay and Gibbons Gardening Services). The police think they have found Scott's lifeless body which Jim must identify. Thankfully, it is not Scott. He later turns up in hospital dazed and confused (and played by Jason Donovan!). On the 13th, Des gets cold feet on his wedding day when Daphne is late. By the time Daphne arrives at the church, Des has run off convinced he is jinxed. Zoe learns that Mike is beaten regularly by his father. Madge and Helen recover her money from Douglas Blake in a brilliant scam. Helen's daughter, Rosemary, visits from New York.

August

Rosemary learns that she was adopted and finally meets her real mother. Zoe becomes Paul's secretary. Shane moves in on Daphne again now she has split from Des. Max goes for a medical and is told he is unfit. He becomes unnervingly nice to the neighbours believing he is about to drop dead of a heart attack. Zoe starts dating Jim. Helen and Shane start the chauffeur service Home James. Andrea Townsend claims her son Bradley is Des's.

September

Helen tries to surprise Nikki by inviting her mum Laura (Helen's sister) to stay, but Nikki and Laura only fight. Daphne shocks Shane by announcing their engagement to everyone. However, Daphne has dinner with Des and it's clear they still have feeling for each other. Jim and Paul argue over Zoe. Clive reveals he's a doctor when he performs a tracheotomy on Lucy on the Robinsons' kitchen table. Eileen returns and vows to prove that Bradley is not Des's son, and she goes to Perth in search of evidence. On the 28th, Scott catches Charlene

Mitchell breaking into her mother's house at Number 24.

October

Eileen returns with proof that Des isn't young Brad's father, but Des is now so fond of the boy that he still wants Andrea and Bradley to hang around. The neighbours have a pancake competition and Helen promises to teach Max so he can beat his pompous sister. But when her ex, Fred Mitchell, arrives Madge isn't worried about the pancakes. Lucy embarrasses Jim and Zoe by asking about sex. Mrs Mangel is seen for the first time complaining in the Coffee Shop. Des hires Clive's Gift of the Gab service to win back Daphne. The Coffee Shop moves to the Lassiter's complex. Tom Ramsay arrives.

November

Scott and Charlene start dating. Zoe announces she's pregnant, but miscarries only a few days later. Des and Daphne finally get it together and set a wedding date. Mrs Mangel moves into Number 32. Tom's old flame Jean Richards arrives.

December

Andrea Townsend makes an old man very happy when she marries Jack Lassiter (who has just sold the hotel to the Daniels Corporation) and leaves with Bradley to start a new life. Nikki leaves to be with her mum when she learns Laura is sick. Graham Gibbons and his family come to stay in the Ape House and he tries to persuade his brother Clive to go back into medicine. On the 22nd, Des and Daphne finally marry. But the happiness turns sour when Shane's car suffers a blow out and crashes killing Tom's girlfriend Jean. A man gives him some brandy after the crash to calm him and then disappears to call an ambulance. When Shane is breathalysed he is over the limit and charged with manslaughter. Shane starts an extensive search for the good samaritan, Alex Carter, and eventually clears his name.

1988

January

Zoe leaves to be with her new love, Tony Chapman. Charlene receives a mysterious phone call and starts skipping school. Des does his back in on their honeymoon, and the Clarkes return home early. Jane Harris moves in with Mrs Mangel at Number 32 and instantly falls for Mike Young. Charlene comes home with a baby and tells Madge it is hers.

February

Charlene confesses that baby Sam is not her son, but her half-brother and she invites his mum Susan (Fred's former mistress) to stay at Number 24. Daphne and Charlene's makeover on Jane bowls Mike over. Madge becomes Paul's secretary, but is moved to The Waterhole when she refuses to get to grips with the computer. Clive feels guilty when he fails to diagnose that Daphne has meningitis. Des fears for the worst when she is hospitalised. Dan

Ramsay arrives and announces that he has left his wife of nearly 50 years, Edna. Ruth Wilson is invited to stay at the Robinsons' when she can't meet her bill at Lassiter's. Madge hires Gift of the Gab to get Dan and Edna back together, but not before Edna has learnt that her marriage was never legal in the first place. Paul announces he is involved in a plan to buy up Ramsay Street and sell the land to a supermarket developer.

March

On the 1st, Dan and Edna finally make it legal. Australian football star Warwick Capper turns up in the Coffee Shop to catch up on old times with his pal Des Clarke (everyone is amazed that Des has such a famous friend). Ray Murphy, a regular at The Waterhole, asks Madge out; she declines. Paul is ostracised by everyone over the supermarket development. Jane and Charlene enter a talent contest and Scott and Mike form a band. Nikki Dennison returns and comes between Jane and Mike, although Mike soon makes it clear he's not interested. Daphne is having difficulty conceiving. Helen learns that her late husband had an affair. Clive proposes to Susan.

April

Susan rejects Clive's offer and starts a secret fling with Paul who is in love with her. He also learns that Terri has killed herself in jail. Warren tries to come between Scott and Charlene. Scott fails to babysit Lucy and she runs off to play and gets trapped down a well. She is found the next day scared and confused, suffering from hysterical blindness. She regains her sight but doesn't tell anyone as she knows Ruth will leave if she can see. Shane flirts with Jane and Mike suspects there might be more than flirting involved when Shane and Jane get lost and spend the night alone in the bush.

May

Clive diagnoses Des's food cravings as sympathetic and announces that Daphne is finally pregnant! Jim buys Scott a car but he crashes it the same day. Mike and Shane fight over Jane. Paul fires Susan when she rejects him. Charlene and Jane play a trick on Scott and Mike which leaves them stark naked on the beach! Paul proposes to Susan who turns him down and leaves town.

June

Shane and Charlene track down Madge's old flame Harold Bishop and invite him to dinner. Scott starts writing for the *Erinsborough News*. Rosemary returns for a brief visit and Henry is finally released from prison.

July

Shane leaves to see Australia on his new motorbike. After a mix-up with one of her paintings, Helen invites Mrs Mangel to sit for her. But Mrs M is less than happy with the unflattering portrait. Nevertheless, she displays it in her hall. Paul gives a job at Lassiter's to his friend from his airline days, Gail Lewis. Harold opens a health shop. Des and Jim start a fitness feud which takes them on a long distance run. Jim falls and injures himself so Des has to seek help. However he gets trapped on a rock in the middle of a river as he can't swim and he is missing for days.

August

The neighbours help Paul out at Lassiter's when a strike grinds the hotel to a stop. The exam results come through and Scott has failed and must retake Year 12. Daphne's father Allen approaches Des and convinces him to let him see Daphne. Harold becomes Rob Lewis's partner in his car repair garage. Henry and Jane start a romance.

September

After rowing with her mother, Charlene moves into the caravan at Lassiter's and Scott is upset when Warren Murphy stays the night. Gail's first husband Jeremy Lord turns up and persuades Rob and Jim to get involved in his next motor racing adventure with a classic car. Mike becomes an intellectual snob now that he's started at university. Scott rescues Charlene from an explosion at the caravan, and Lucy (now played by Sasha Close) returns from Europe.

October

Jeremy dies in a racing accident. Charlene's bid to earn millions selling Liquid Beauty furniture polish door-to-door turns sour when the neighbours discover the polish's other use – as glue! Charlene must then pay for all the damaged furniture out of her earnings from her new job at Rob's garage. Mrs Mangel loses her memory after falling off a ladder and is temporarily lovely! Scott proposes to Charlene after their parents refuse to let them live together. Jim is furious at the news. Des faints when he watches a childbirth video. On the 25th, Paul and Gail marry to gain a contract from Japanese businessman, Mr Udugawa.

November

Cousin Hilary arrives for Scott and Charlene's wedding and stays with Paul and Gail. She is suspicious when she sees they sleep in separate bedrooms. Reverend Sampson declares Scott and Charlene man and wife on the 8th. Rob has been squandering profits at the garage. Beverly Marshall meets Jim and there is an instant attraction. Henry and Madge change their surname to Ramsay.

December

Mike tells Jane about Megan, a girl he has met studying in Canberra. Jamie Clarke is born during a picnic on the 6th. Henry introduces Ramsay Street to his new girlfriend Melanie Pearson, whose annoying laugh gets on everyone's nerves.

1989

January

Amanda Harris visits Jane and makes her remove her make-up and wear her hair in pigtails again.

Harold is distraught when he mistakenly eats ham in soup served at the Coffee Shop. Scott and Charlene have money worries. Bev's ex, Ewan, turns up in Erinsborough and it looks like he might tempt her away from Jim. Allen Lawrence arrives unexpectedly at Jamie's christening.

February

Paul and Gail kiss spontaneously after celebrating a success at work. Money is mysteriously given to baby Jamie. It is from Allen whose money Daphne had rejected while she was pregnant because of her father's lust for a grandson, rather than a granddaughter. It is decided that the money will be put into a trust fund. Jane becomes the Lassiter's Girl. Harold breaks both arms and moves in with Des to get help with the little things in life. Gail confides in Beverly that she is in love with Paul. Allen tells his daughter he is dying, and Daphne leaves Ramsay Street to care for her father.

March

Scott and Jane spend a lot of time together as she helps him study for his HSC. He kisses her on Charlene's birthday and their passion is witnessed by Henry. Shamefully, Jane leaves town for a business conference and Mike fights with Scott for making Jane go away. Lucy develops a crush on Mike. Scott resits his exams. Jane returns for a showdown with Charlene and makes Charlene realise she still loves Scott and the pair reunite. Madge accidentally runs over Bouncer while learning to drive.

Eileen Clarke and Mrs Mangel join the local bowling club. Tony Romeo starts work in the Coffee Shop. Eileen comes face to face with the man who left her all those years ago, Des's dad Malcolm. After a massive row with Gail, Paul admits to his family that they have an arranged marriage. Convinced that Paul doesn't love her, Gail makes plans to leave. At the last minute during the reopening of The Waterhole, Scott convinces his big brother to run after Gail, which he does and Paul and Gail embrace. Jane, Scott and Mike are lost at sea and Scott swims ashore to find help. Gail reveals to Paul that she can't have children.

Malcolm proposes to Eileen and they plan a second wedding. Scott gets a full-time job with the local paper after passing his HSC. Helen moves out of Number 26 to a flat which is believed to be haunted (the ghost turns out to be a cat). Malcolm upsets Eileen on the morning of their wedding on the 17th and she calls it off. On the 23rd, Jim and Beverly tie the knot and Paul and Gail make use of the minister and take their marriage vows again.

Des's half-sister Sally Wells arrives and starts work in the Coffee Shop where she argues with Tony. Beverly takes to domestic chores badly and burns the meal at her first dinner party. Helen is persuaded to move back in to take care of the kitchen! Charlene finds a valuable coin in a car she is fixing. Helen and Beverly witness a car crash. Bev rushes to the scene to see if she can help and is shocked to find the casualties are Gail and Daphne returning from Allen's funeral. Des is distraught but believes Daphne will pull through. Gail comes out of her coma and remembers the licence plate of the car that caused the smash.

July

Daphne dies on the 3rd after waking briefly to tell Des that she loved him. Millionaire car salesman Lou Carpenter arrives at the Ramsay house to declare his intention to marry old flame Madge. Naturally this ruffles Harold's feathers and the two men fight. Mike goes after the driver of the car that killed Daphne and his actions land him in court. Jim's partner in the engineering firm Ross Warner, is proved to be fraudulent, and Jim leaves the business. Mrs Mangel gets a new job as a lollipop lady. Rob introduces his fiancée, Gloria, to Gail.

August

Malcolm is seen winning a European holiday in a TV quiz show and he invites Sally and Eileen to share his prize. David Bishop arrives for his dad's wedding to Madge on the 18th.

September

Charlene starts taking driving lessons from Steve Fisher, and Scott suspects her of sleeping with him. Bouncer decides to go and live with Mrs Mangel. Paul's old flame Nina visits Lassiter's and reveals that Paul is the father of her daughter Amy. Gail frets that this means that Paul will no longer want to try for a baby with her. Gail, who is adopted, tracks down her real father and Rob is upset until Gail tells him that he's the father she really loves. Englishman John Worthington takes an interest in Mrs Mangel.

October

Jane develops a crush on Des, but when he goes on and on about Daphne, she realises he's not ready for another relationship yet. Bronwyn is employed as Jamie's new nanny. Dan arrives from Brisbane and offers Scott and Charlene a house as a present. The young couple decide to accept the generous offer and they get nostalgic about their years together.

November

Charlene leaves Ramsay Street in her car on the 1st while Scott stays behind until he can secure work in Brisbane. Henry catches the graffiti artist who has been plaguing the neighbourhood. But Helen is so impressed with Nick Page's artistic talents that she takes him in and gives him art lessons. Todd clashes badly with Nick and the two lads have vicious fights at Number 26. Henry and Jane track down her uncle, Joe Mangel, who arrives for his mum's wedding. Bronwyn's sister Sharon and aunty Edie arrive for a visit. Gail is made the manager of Lassiter's.

December

Ramsay Street is struck by a plague of mosquitoes! Sharon and Nick start a budding romance. Jane finds herself mediating between Mrs Mangel and Joe.

1990

January

Harold is a hero when he saves Bronwyn from a fire. Paul gets a dressing down from Helen who tells him he is mean and uncaring. Scott matchmakes between Henry and Bronwyn who instantly hit it off. Bev miscarries after being involved in a car accident. Gail's IVF treatment has been successful and she announces she is expecting triplets! Harold becomes Des's partner in the Coffee Shop and Mike starts work as a teacher at Erinsborough High.

February

Mrs Mangel marries John Worthington on the 1st and they leave for a new life in England the following day. Mike discovers one of his pupils Jessie Ross has troubles at home and he takes a keen interest in her. Todd falls under the wing of local bad boy, Skinner. Mike is caught comforting Jessie and is suspended. Joe's ex-wife Noeline dumps their son Toby at Number 32. Bronwyn moves into Number 24 to live in sin with Henry despite Harold's disapproval.

March

Joe and Jim both design go-karts for Toby and Todd to race. Helen suffers a stroke and is hospitalised. The neighbours celebrate Christmas while Paul tries to stave off a takeover bid for Lassiter's. Nick is furious when Sharon starts work as a nude artists' model.

April

Harold's daughter Kerry turns up on his doorstep with her daughter Sky. Gail gets upset when Paul continues to put Lassiter's before her and the babies she's expecting. Joe and Kerry notice each other and start dating. Jane's American boyfriend Mark proposes to her and she accepts, but when Mike returns he lets it be known he wants her back.

May

Nick is expelled from school. Paul and Gail go on holiday in an effort to make things work. Mike starts dating a girl called Jenny Owens. Jim and Bev argue over her desire to have a baby.

June

Jenny leaves Mike whose attentions turn once again to Jane, who is now interested in Des again.

July

Nick starts printing T-shirts to make some extra cash. Des starts learning Japanese to improve his job prospects. Scott leaves on the 24th to be with Charlene in Brisbane. Bev is having problems getting pregnant and decides to adopt. Matt Williams arrives to see his mother, Hilary.

August

At Mike's 21st birthday party, he and Jane become close and he thinks they may get back together. Joe starts a professional video service and practises on the neighbours. Hilary starts looking out for Sharon who is becoming like a surrogate daughter to her.

September

Sharon makes herself ill by dieting. Matt asks Hilary to tell the Robinsons that he is her illegitimate son. Jane is knocked down by a car and ends up in hospital. When she would rather be comforted by Des than Mike, Mike guesses that there's something going on between them. Nick and Matt have a fight over Sharon. Mike flirts with Bronwyn in a bid to make Jane jealous, but finds that he actually really likes her.

October

Bronwyn chooses Henry over Mike who has also lost out to Des who is now engaged to Jane. Des and Jane start to argue over their wedding plans. Mike, feeling sorry for himself, has a one-night stand.

November

Matt decides to take Hilary's surname now that they have got to know each other. Bev goes to Adelaide to see her sister Annette who is having serious problems with her husband Bob. Henry gets a job as a grave-digger. Gail, heavily pregnant and fed up with playing second fiddle to Lassiter's, walks out on Paul. Jane learns that Nell is poorly in England and she leaves Des to take care of her grandmother.

On the 4th, Joe and Kerry marry in a butterfly house. Todd announces he is in love with his new girlfriend Melissa Jarrett. Clive returns to Ramsay Street briefly and finds himself offering comfort to a devastated Paul. Melanie becomes Des's lodger and cheers him up. Todd fails to impress Melissa's parents when their meeting turns into a social disaster. Henry makes his debut as a radio DJ.

1991

January

Hilary starts dating high school principal Mr Muir. Lucy returns during the school vacation and falls for Nick who is still living with the Robinsons. Toby meets Lochy and together they investigate a mysterious haunted house. Paul's bad moods are not helped when Gail writes to him and asks for maintenance for the triplets. Des returns from Perth with a new attitude, sideburns and a career as a stockbroker. He intends returning to the West coast and his new girlfriend as soon as he can sell Number 28.

February

Henry leaves in tears on the 1st to take up a job as a DJ in New Zealand. Cody Willis makes her first appearance as Melissa's friend at school. The neighbours celebrate Christmas in the sun and Sharon gets severe sunstroke in the heat. Bev fosters baby Rhys and becomes overly attached.

March

A mysterious Linda Giles rents Number 22 who causes much confusion until it is revealed that she is in fact two people – identical twins Caroline and Christina Alessi. Madge and Harold leave Erinsborough for a round the world trip. Kerry wants to move the Mangel clan to the country, but Toby and Joe persuade her to stay. Josh asks Melissa out on a date. Bev gets neurotic when Rhys is taken away from her. She throws herself into her work and makes herself too busy to remember Todd's birthday. Jim and Bev's marriage looks set to end in divorce. While working at Lassiter's, Matt meets Barry Dwyer – his real father.

April

Lochy's older brother Ryan takes Bronwyn to the school dance unaware that she is engaged to Henry. He falls for her and is disappointed when he learns the truth. Jim and Bev's constant arguments upset Helen so much that she moves out. In England, Madge and Harold meet Rosemary Daniels who introduces them to Lord Legerwood. Nick also heads for England after gaining a scholarship to a prestigious art college. Beverly's ex, Ewan, returns to the fray, but this time it seems he might really take her away from Jim.

May

Joe believes Sky is a child genius, but actually it's just Toby playing a trick on him. Dorothy Burke moves next door with Ryan and kicks up a fuss with

Joe about the position of a fence. Harold and Madge return with Eddie Buckingham in tow. Eddie is swiftly given a job at the Coffee Shop. Todd gets in with the wrong crowd again when he starts bike scrambling.

June

Bev and Jim finally separate and she takes Todd to live with her at the surgery. Joe has to tell Toby that his mother Noeline has died. The lad is depressed for a while, but bounces back and decides that from now on he will call Kerry 'mum'. Harold is encouraged to run for the local council – with some competition from Madge. Todd announces he wants to stay with Jim and be in Ramsay Street with his friends. Caroline and Christina both reveal that they fancy Paul, although Caroline thinks her boss doesn't take her seriously.

July

Chrissie however thinks Caroline doesn't take her seriously, and takes lessons in business practice from Des. Madge is elected to the local council. Melissa dumps Todd to go out with Josh, but Todd consoles himself in the arms of Cody. Josh saves the day when he foils a virus on the Lassiter's computer.

August

Madge's niece Gemma comes to live at Number 24. Rosemary drops in to visit her mum while in town on business. Jim and Caroline start to see each other, much to everyone else's consternation – especially Bev's who is now living with Ewan. Bouncer goes missing! Although everyone fears the worst, the pooch was having the time of his life with Clarrie McLachlan's dog Rosie – the dogs even married in a dream sequence! Kerry tells the world she is pregnant and it seems the Mangels are the happiest family in Erinsborough. Mel starts a relationship with an older man, Roger.

September

Des sells his shares in the Coffee Shop to Madge. Mel meets Roger's fourteen-year-old daughter Tania and fails miserably in the potential stepmum stakes. Paul and Chrissie start dating after smooching at a party. Gemma and Matt start a relationship. Des employs Cody's dad, Doug Willis, to do some construction work at Number 28, and ends up selling the house to him. Kerry encourages Melissa to be an environmental activist and they free the mice from the school science labs.

October

Jim and Helen worry about Bev who has become neurotic and they encourage her to return to her family in Adelaide, which she does, taking Todd with her. An old travelling friend of Kerry's, Amber Martin, turns up and tells Kerry that she has become 'safe and suburban' and she encourages Kerry to return to her militant activist ways. She goes on a protest and to Joe's horror is arrested. He is therefore loath to let her attend a protest against poachers, but agrees to accompany her to stop her getting into any trouble. Tragically, on the 22nd, Kerry is killed by a poacher's stray bullet. Caroline starts dating new resident Adam Willis. Paul returns from a business trip to Argentina with Isabella Lopez who he intends to marry. Todd is found hiding in Cody's bedroom – he has run away from Adelaide to be with her. Jim lets him stay on at Number 26.

November

Jim and Adam find themselves in an absurd fight for Caroline. Eddie returns to England when he hears his father is ill. Melissa becomes jealous of the new girl in Josh's life, the mysterious Katrina. It transpires that Katrina is Josh's violin teacher on whom the boy has a crush. Chrissie tries desperately to discredit Isabella, fearing Paul may be out of her grasp forever. Eventually she proves Isabella's sole interest in Paul is his passport (she had intended to marry him in a bid to avoid a difficult life back home). Chrissie expects Paul to now fall into her arms, and is gutted when he tells her he's given up on women because they're too much hassle! Des finally leaves for his new life in Perth. Ryan becomes belligerent and joins the army. Joe is dealt a body blow when Sky's natural father, Eric Jensen, announces he wants custody of his daughter.

December

Lonely Jim joins a video dating agency. Chrissie takes over Mel's job at Lassiter's in a bid to be closer to Paul. Melanie offers to marry Joe if it will help him win custody of Sky. Paul and Doug develop plans for a guest house on Lassiter's land. Melissa starts a frantic search to find the 'phantom kisser' after she is kissed by a mysterious man at a party.

1992

January

Dorothy receives a marriage proposal from John Brice but she turns him down and reveals to Helen that she is already married. Paul gets so jealous when he sees Chrissie with Rory Marsden that he finally tells Chrissie how he feels about her. Pretty soon they are discussing marriage. After Pam finds condoms from sex education classes in Cody's school bag she assumes her daughter is already sleeping with Todd. She bans the teenagers from seeing each other, and Todd and Cody run away. Glen Donnelly turns up on Jim's doorstep and announces he is his son. Tom Ramsay returns to inspect Gemma's boyfriend Matt, and when Gemma is hospitalised after an accident he blames Matt. Joe kidnaps Sky from Eric Jensen when he fears he will lose the custody battle.

February

After collapsing with a fever, Cody is brought back to Ramsay Street, but Todd stays away. Toby is caught ringing expensive joke phone lines. Tensions between Glen and Paul ease slightly when Paul invites his half-brother to his wedding. Doug is angry when Pam states her desire to return to nursing. Joe loses the custody battle, but after a week or so of caring for Sky, Eric returns her to Ramsay Street

218

realising that Joe makes the better father. Paul and Chrissie wed on the 19th, and after a day of confusion bridesmaid Melanie ends up on the honeymoon cruise!

March

On holiday, the Willis family are caught in a bush fire and Cody is missing. Doug and Pam presume the worst when the emergency services tell them they have spotted a body. Thankfully Cody is found alive and well the next day. The neighbours begin to suspect that there may be more than friendship between Jim and Dorothy. Melanie starts a quest to find Joe Mangel the perfect date. Gemma's ex-boyfriend Aidan turns up and makes it quite clear that he still loves her. This leads to arguments for Matt and Gemma. Ryan announces he's joining the army. Madge has an operation on her vocal cords which could leave permanent damage, but of course it doesn't.

April

Dorothy's husband Colin is released from prison after serving a sentence for accountancy fraud and tells his wife he wants to start again. She believes him and he moves into Number 30. Lucy arrives home from boarding school and takes a shine to Glen, unaware that he is her half-brother. Madge and Harold matchmake between Gemma and Adam who they consider to be 'suitable'. The Willises have severe financial problems and tensions build at Number 28 as Pam takes on the housework as well as her nursing studies. Joe is shocked when he catches Colin Burke in bed with Rosemary Daniels while window cleaning at Lassiter's. When tests show that Chrissie isn't pregnant she doesn't have the heart to tell enthusiastic Paul her news. So she pretends she is pregnant and sets about getting that way very quickly. Paul is a little confused by her unexplained passion.

May

Madge clashes with Paul when she makes The Waterhole a no-smoking pub. Paul soon reverses this decision in the name of profit. The Willises' money problems are so severe that Doug announces they will have to move to a smaller house. Harold arrives home from a trip with the scouts a broken man after a boy in his care died. It seems the devout Christian has lost his faith in God. Bouncer is mistaken for a dangerous dog and comes close to being put down. Josh reveals that he has been living in a garage. The feuds between Paul and Glen, and Madge and Dorothy both take a turn for the worse. However, Dorothy soon becomes less interested in her bickering with Madge when she is told she has breast cancer. She is quickly treated and undergoes a mastectomy.

June

Melanie's attempts to find Joe a partner lead her to scour the lonely hearts ads and persuade her landlord to visit singles bars. Chrissie finally announces she's pregnant, but when she nearly miscarries Paul vows to put the office on the back burner and work from home to take care of her. Glen and Gemma split, as do Adam and Caroline, and pretty soon

Adam and Gemma start dating. Helen meets Michael Daniels, her late husband's cousin, in the doctor's surgery. While out driving Joe discovers a body in the road and manages to brake just before he hits it. Josh starts to woo Lucy by giving her expensive earrings; however, he doesn't tell her about his new job – as a stripper!

July

Joe is a victim of an evil campaign to frame him for the road accident. Michael proposes to Helen and she accepts. Gemma nearly loses her job at the animal sanctuary when she joins a protest against the use of animals in circuses. Chrissie and Lucy vie for Paul's approval in the bid to be the new Lassiter's Girl; meanwhile Todd vies for Cody with school bully Darren Wood. Todd wins her over only to lose her when she leaves to study in America. Josh is embarrassed when he is booked to perform at Helen's hen night and is mortified when he is unmasked. Shortly before their wedding on the 28th, Michael mysteriously tries to call off the wedding. Jim persuades him to go through with it but starts to get suspicious of Helen's new Mr Wonderful. Harold suffers a heart attack which makes Madge overprotective of him. Pam and Doug fly to Bagee where their son Brad is being held on drugs charges. Joe realises that the girl of his dreams is right under his nose – it's Melanie!

August

Joe's heart sinks when he realises Melanie has fallen for Simon Hunter, a client of Lassiter's. Gaby Willis

221

arrives home from studying in Japan and quickly relieves some of her parents' money worries by tricking one of their debtors that she was the family lawyer – and he quickly hands over a cheque for $10,000. Jim is depressed when the news comes through that his divorce from Beverly is final. He is saddened further when he catches his sons, Glen and Paul, in a fist fight. Pam and Doug bring Brad home who goes surfing at dawn the next day. Melanie accepts Simon's proposal of marriage, and although Joe is heart-broken, he doesn't say a word. Madge and Harold rent Number 24 to Brenda Riley who will house-sit while they embark on a tour of Australia. Glen's ex-girlfriend Karen turns up and is eight months pregnant. She claims the baby is Glen's and he offers to marry her. However, when it comes to exchanging vows in the registry office, Karen breaks down and confesses the baby isn't Glen's after all – she was just looking for a father for her baby. Doug's guest-house deal with Paul is under threat when Felicity Brent – a local councillor – says she will vote against the planning decision. Madge arranges for Joe to go on the TV show *Dream Date*. While Helen is on her honeymoon, Jim discovers that Michael is a bigamist. Melanie accompanies Joe to *Dream Date* for moral support, but typically Melanie screws up and ends up being a contestant! Although she tries to disguise her voice, Joe still picks her and the newly matched couple win a holiday for two.

September

On holiday, Melanie realises that she is also in love with Joe and the couple plan to marry. Paul and

Caroline get stuck in the bush overnight when their car breaks down and it's clear there's a certain chemistry between them. Dorothy runs for the local council. Helen is distraught when she hears Michael is already married, even though his first wife had been hospitalised for many years. Adam leaves to join Gemma in Newcastle while his sister Gaby opens her boutique, Gabrielle, at Lassiter's. On holiday, Harold disappears and is presumed drowned when he goes missing on a clifftop. Brenda Riley sets her sights on Doug Willis, who is flattered by her attention but not tempted. After an armed robbery at Lassiter's, Paul attempts fraud by claiming excess losses from the insurers. Joe discovers that Melanie once had a brief fling with Paul and finds this information difficult to deal with.

October

Lucy starts dating Guy Carpenter, Brenda's nephew, who has moved into Number 24. On the 5th, the whole of Erinsborough celebrate as Joe and Melanie finally tie the knot. Madge leaves for Brisbane to be with Charlene while she grieves for Harold. Todd receives a letter from Cody telling him she's found someone else. Melanie and Joe return from their honeymoon to learn that Mrs Mangel has been taken ill and they decide to fly to England to see her. Gaby starts dating Glen and Josh sees 'creepy' Phoebe Bright for the first time. Pam is worried when she fears she may be pregnant again. Number 32 is put up for auction and Helen buys it. Rosemary returns and offers Caroline a job with her in New York.

Doug takes on an elderly craftsman called Garth Kirby who soon becomes ill. Caroline uncovers a plot within the Daniels Corporation to oust Paul, and out of loyalty she tells him. He thanks her by offering her old job back at the renamed Robinson Corporation. In her absence Paul had employed Martin Tyrell to manage Lassiter's, and on her return Caroline clashes badly with Martin, a married man with kids. However their friction soon causes sparks of passion! Brad Willis falls in love with Paige Sneddon unaware that she is only after his surfboard designs. Chrissie gives birth to baby Andrew on the 10th. Caroline is devastated when Martin goes back to his wife.

December

Todd has an awkward reunion with his dad Bob who ends up squatting in the vacant Number 32. Josh, Brad and Lucy go on holiday to Queensland where they meet Beth Brennan and her brother David. Lou Carpenter arrives in Ramsay Street to see his little sister Brenda – he gets a surprise when Madge, his old flame, also comes back to Erinsborough after her stay in Queensland. Glen falls from the roof of The Waterhole while trying to fix a banner. His injuries leave him paralysed and he threatens to sue Paul for damages. If Glen wins it will bankrupt Paul who becomes depressed, even suicidal. In Queensland, Josh and Brad enter into a battle for Beth while Lucy enjoys a fling with David.

1993

January

Lou and Guy call a truce and bury their differences. The Willises have finally had enough of the awful Faye Hudson and her meddling ways and ask her to leave. She does – and promptly rents Number 32. Garth Kirby is terminally ill and in a lot of pain. Pam and Doug visit him daily and he asks both of them to put him out of his misery. Glen is angry and full of hate after his accident and ditches Gaby. He finds some comfort with ex-girlfriend Karen and they leave Ramsay Street together. Phoebe has a showdown with her overbearing father. Her worries are added to when it is revealed that Toby Mangel has a crush on her. Jim Robinson is under attack when Faye Hudson decides he's the man for her!

February

Brenda's estranged husband Roy returns and they reunite. A severely depressed Paul disappears. Chrissie has to face the awful prospect that he might have died when the police discover a body that could be his in a hotel fire. Phoebe realises she'd much rather be with Todd than Josh and sends him a love letter. Brad and Lucy start dating, although things aren't serious. So when Beth turns up in Ramsay Street she's still in with a chance with Brad. Pam goes to visit Garth and finds his lifeless body. Soon she is arrested for his murder as the police believe she aided euthanasia.

March

Faye's son Cameron rides into Ramsay Street on his motorbike. Cameron is a lawyer and quickly finds work defending his aunt Pam against the murder charge. Things go wrong for Brad and Lucy when she drives his car whilst under the influence of alcohol and ends in a lake. Both are unharmed but Lucy is severely shaken and vows to grow up.

April

Gaby's boutique goes up in flames because of Faye's carelessness. Faye is too worried to confess to the crime until weeks later when the evidence forces her to confess. Lucy and Beth enter into a bitter battle for Brad's affections. Todd and Phoebe make a commitment to each other and sleep together for the first time. Marco Alessi arrives only to become privy to the illicit romance between his cousin Caroline and her brother-in-law Paul. Caroline realises that she can no longer live under the same roof as Paul without hurting her sister and so she leaves impulsively for Milan. Chrissie is very suspicious of her sister's sudden departure. Doug's photo appears in the *Erinsborough News*.

May

Beth and Marco kiss briefly, but it leads to nothing even though Marco hopes for more. Jill Weir spots Doug's photo in the paper and takes a shine to him. She soon appears in Ramsay Street looking for him. Chrissie learns about Paul's dalliance with Caroline and throws him out. Beth reveals she is seeing an older man – Rod Baker. Rick Alessi joins his big brother in Ramsay Street and Marco persuades Dorothy to let him attend Erinsborough High. Lou proposes to Madge who politely turns him down explaining that she is still grieving for Harold. Phoebe gingerly tells Todd that she's pregnant. Lucy wins her battle with Beth for Brad and plans to move in with him. Jill Weir's constant interest in Doug starts to unsettle him.

June

Paul decides he will fight for custody of Andrew when Chrissie refuses him access to his son. Phoebe decides she'd like to keep the baby, but is persuaded by the 'older and wiser' women of Ramsay Street that she is throwing her future away, so she changes her mind and decides to terminate the pregnancy. Beth starts work for Doug on the building sites and encounters plenty of male chauvinism. Lucy leaves Brad and Ramsay Street for a modelling career in Singapore. Cameron starts dating glamorous older woman, Jacqueline Summers. While Phoebe attends the abortion clinic, Todd decides he wants to keep the baby after all and rushes to the clinic. In his haste he is knocked over by a van and taken to hospital where he later dies. At his funeral, Bob Landers takes Helen hostage. Julie and her family return for the funeral but arrive too late. Paul declares his love for Chrissie at a special service where they retake their marriage vows before leaving for a new life in Hawaii. Chrissie's aunt and uncle Cathy and Benito Alessi move into Number 22 with their sons Marco and Rick.

July

Gaby dates Simon Hunter, who was once engaged to Melanie Pearson. He seems like a nice guy but when they go away for the weekend together he tries to rape Gaby. When Doug and Brad learn of this they attack him, so when Gaby threatens to report him, Simon retaliates that he will sue Doug for assault. In the end all charges are dropped. Bob Landers takes Phoebe hostage. The siege is ended when Brad rescues Phoebe but is shot in the process. He is comforted by Beth, who asks him to sleep with her so she can overcome her memories of abuse at the hands of her mother's lover. One night, when they are left alone in the middle of a rainstorm, they make love.

August

Cathy reveals that she had her first child, a baby girl, adopted when she was only sixteen. Marco takes the news badly and vows to track down his long lost sister. He eventually finds her but she doesn't want to know him. Later, her curiosity gets the better of her and she turns up in Ramsay Street and has dinner with her natural parents. Things are strained between Brad and Beth after their night of passion, but they soon overcome their embarrassment and start dating properly. Jim joins Gaby and the Alessi boys in a bike race, even though they tease him about his age. Their teasing leads Jim to train harder and he ends up collapsing with chest pains. Luckily Pam drives past and helps him. She is convinced he has had a heart attack. Sadly she can't convince him to go to hospital for some tests, and sure enough he collapses again. This time even Jim is scared and he agrees to take things easy.

September

While grieving at Todd's graveside, Phoebe meets record store manager Stephen Gottlieb who is mourning the death of his girlfriend. Stephen is keen that he and Phoebe should date, but she still feels bad about Todd. She holds a seance in the Robinson house trying to get in touch with Todd's spirit in order to get his blessing to start dating Stephen. Michael Martin arrives and starts his campaign of terror against his stepmum Julie. Jim and Pam become close and Doug suspects them of having an affair. He eventually falls for the charms of Jill Weir and they have a one-night stand. He sees it as a harmless fling – but she wants more and returns to Ramsay Street to make sure she gets it. At one point she even threatens to kill herself if he won't choose her over Pam. Pam is so distraught that she throws herself at Jim and they kiss passionately before he breaks it off saying he won't do anything while she is still married to his friend.

October

Stephen proposes to Phoebe and she accepts even though she isn't really in love with him. Rick and Debbie win a trip to London to see Michael Jackson in concert. They are well aware that their parents wouldn't let them take the trip alone, so Marco and Helen act as escorts. Marco soon goes missing when loan sharks track him down and he is never seen again, although he leaves a note saying he will be all right. Helen is taken ill leaving Rick and Debbie free to explore London unaccompanied. They meet Terry, a boy with leukaemia, who is a big fan of Michael Jackson and end up giving him their tickets. They later appear on TV to talk about their charitable deed, but land themselves in trouble when the show is screened in Australia and their parents realise they have been together. An era finally comes to an end when the last of the Ramsays – Madge – packs her bags and goes to live in Brisbane with her daughter Charlene. Beth and Hannah are trapped in a fire at a cottage, but they are rescued at the last minute by Brad who braves the flames.

November

Now that Lou is alone he decides to sharpen up his image. Still pining for Madge he takes up with a glamorous blonde called Annalise who he believes is 21 years old. But when Annalise's mum Fiona arrives, Lou is disgusted to learn Annalise is still only seventeen! Rick and Debbie find themselves grounded after their London trip, but they sneak time together running the school radio station. Naturally they cause trouble! They manage to evacuate the building claiming it's on fire, and they really land themselves in trouble when they embarrass Mr Knotts by saying he fancies Mrs Burke. Dorothy in fact falls for education inspector Tom Merrick and she leaves Erinsborough to take up a new post with him in the country. She also takes Toby with her. Stephen's stag night takes a dramatic turn when Phoebe prematurely goes into labour. The wedding is cancelled and Stephen fears that Phoebe will not marry him if their tiny daughter dies. Baby Hope pulls through and they agree to marry later in the month, on the 27th. Brad beats his sister Gaby to the job as manager of The Waterhole, but Gaby is consoled when she is given the job as Philip's secretary at Lassiter's. Cameron gets himself into trouble with a crook called Heywood. When Heywood threatens to kill him he agrees to become his company lawyer and investigate the fire at the cottage, for which he suspects Michael Martin is responsible.

December

Michael's hate campaign against Julie takes a serious turn when he leaves her to drown after doping her with sleeping pills. She is rescued by Debbie and Rick. Jim believes there is no need for him to stay in Ramsay Street now all his kids have left home and he makes plans to move elsewhere. But the neighbours launch 'Operation Jim' to deter any potential buyers for Number 26 and in the end Jim agrees to stay put. Brad buys Beth a friendship ring, but when she thinks it is an engagement ring he doesn't have the heart to put her straight and finds himself making wedding plans. Gaby reveals that she has been writing to Doug's dad Bert and Pam invites him to stay – much to Doug's disgust as he fell out with his father years ago. While out surfing, Brad meets a mysterious girl horse-riding on the beach. There is an instant attraction between them but she leaves before they even exchange names.

January

Brad is shocked when the girl from the beach rides into Ramsay Street and is revealed to be Lou's daughter Lauren. Beth becomes good friends with Lauren but can't understand why Brad won't see Lauren. Beth has no idea that Brad is trying to deny his attraction. Gaby starts an on-off-on again relationship with new arrival, schoolteacher Wayne Duncan. She also gets involved at work when she suspects Philip is cheating on Julie. In the end his 'missing' hours are explained by regular visits to the gym. But Gaby is still suspicious of his dealing with an agency that she believes is an escort agency. In fact, Philip has hired a detective to try to find Michael. Helen is mugged by tearaway Greg. She is deeply shaken by the crime but Jim eventually persuades her to get out and takes her to The Waterhole where she comes face to face with her attacker. Instead of insisting on calling the police, Helen invites Greg to live with her so she can rehabilitate him. Debbie is severely embarrassed when her stepmum Julie decides to return to school. Jill Weir returns and this time she's after Jim. However, Jim is not interested as he is conducting a secret romance. Helen demands to know the identity of Jim's other half.

February

Brad and Lauren can deny their feelings no longer and make love in secret on the beach. Financial problems force Stephen and Phoebe to take in a lodger, the suspect Russell Butler. Jim reveals that he is in love with Annalise's mother, Fiona Hartman. Julie is disgusted when Jim gives Fiona a pair of her mother Anne's earrings. Helen is equally disgusted and moves in with Julie at Number 32. Annalise is shocked to learn that her father is still alive. Fiona had always told her that her dad had died when she was little, and this is further proof that Fiona is a manipulative person who could spell disaster for Jim. Benito goes to Sydney for a job interview and takes Cathy and Rick with him: Rick meets Michael, and so Debbie and Philip also make the trip to Sydney to see him.

March

Plans are afoot for Brad and Beth's wedding, but the arrival of Beth's mum Bunny unsettles things as she disapproves of Brad. Jim collapses and dies of a heart attack. Fiona is witness to his death but instead of calling an ambulance she seizes her opportunity and calls Jim's banker and transfers his money into her account. She later returns to Number 26 with Rosemary Daniels to 'discover' Jim's body. The neighbours soon realise her story doesn't add up and in the end they actually accuse her of murdering Jim. She shoots through before anyone learns the truth. Lauren fears she may be pregnant by Brad, but a visit to the doctor reveals she has chlamydia. Helen misses Jim so much she turns to the bottle for comfort. On the morning of her wedding, Beth spots Brad and Lauren together and realises what's been going on. When it comes to saying her vows she calls the wedding off. Brad and Lauren continue to date

233

in secret. Michael turns up on the doorstep of Number 32 but Julie refuses to let him in. When Philip returns home a few hours later he finds Michael unconscious on the doorstep. He is furious at Julie for turning his sick son away and asks for a divorce.

April

Lauren and Brad are finally rumbled when Gaby catches them kissing in Number 22 when she shows prospective tenants, the Lims, the house. When Russell tries to snatch baby Hope from Phoebe, Stephen realises it's time to do something about their lodger from hell and arranges for a gang of bikers to 'persuade' Russell to leave. However, they pick on Wayne by mistake and the schoolteacher is beaten to a pulp and left for dead. He recovers but then seeks revenge. When the gang leader, Cactus, is killed Wayne is the number one suspect and is arrested for the murder. Julie proves to hold some very racist views when Hannah becomes friends with new neighbour, Chinese immigrant Tommy Lim. Helen reads some old love letters of Anne's and learns that Jim was not Julie's natural father. Debbie starts seeing Lassiter's chef Harvey Johnson and Rick calls an end to their relationship.

May

Julie goes to Queensland to search for her real dad, Roger Bannon. When she comes face to face with Roger she is shocked to find he is almost the same age as her – he is actually Roger Bannon Jnr, her half-brother. She is disgusted when he comes on to her but even more disgusted when she learns that she is the product of a rape. She returns to Ramsay Street but tells no one what she has learnt. She feels she is dirty and tells Philip she wants a divorce. He moves into Lassiter's while Debbie and Hannah stay at Number 32. The Waterhole explodes and Stephen is trapped inside. His injuries from the blast leave him paralysed. He decides that Phoebe would have a better chance of happiness if they were apart and he tells his wife that their marriage is over. However, they realise they love each other before it's too late and vow to stay together. Julie starts work at the car yard so she can support Hannah. Michael's enemy Darren Starke from the Detention Centre is released and vows to cause trouble for Debbie.

June

Helen's depression deepens when she learns that a friend of hers has died. Doug's company debts mean he is forced to sell out to a bigger company. Darren arrives in Ramsay Street under an assumed identity and sets about wooing Debbie. He quickly succeeds and leads her astray into shop-lifting and joy-riding. Darren's mum Cheryl also arrives and falls head over heels for Lou, doing everything in her power to win him over. Cathy returns briefly to check on Rick. She is much happier when Lou agrees to take him in. Philip starts a subdued affair with Beth after Julie makes it clear their marriage is over. Brad's gambling causes a rift between him and Lauren and he leaves Ramsay Street to take a job on a cruise ship. Stephen's hope in the future is renewed when he manages to catch a frisbee with his bad arm while playing in the park. His spirits are lifted further when his compensation cheque arrives. However, he suffers a relapse when he comes face to face with his older brother Mark who has been masquerading as a French chef at Lassiter's. Julie is so depressed about the conditions surrounding her birth and the state of her marriage that she takes an overdose. She survives, but Beth persuades Philip that he must move back in with his wife to take care of the children. In Brad's absence, Lauren starts a passionate affair with Connor Cleary.

July

Convinced her marriage is over, Julie calls in the lawyers. She also starts therapy to talk about her father. With Rick's help Michael breaks out of jail in an attempt to save Debbie from getting involved in a petrol station raid. They arrive just too late and Michael is shot in the chest. He survives, and Philip makes plans to start a new life with his children in Perth. Annalise and Gaby continue their feud and fight over Mark Gottlieb. Connor asks Lauren to go with him to Hong Kong, but she turns him down and calls their relationship off out of duty to Brad. Cheryl proposes to Lou, but he declines her offer. Pam notices how down Helen is and decides to throw her a surprise birthday party. Brad returns from his trip with a surprise – Lucy! She is to be the special guest at Helen's party. Helen has an extra treat when Paul also returns home for the occasion. The party brings joy for all concerned – Paul gives Gaby the job as manager of Lassiter's, Stephen takes his first steps since the accident, and Julie and Philip kiss and make up after she reveals to him the truth about her father and why she's been so difficult lately. Helen tells everyone that her birthday wish has come true!

ROLL CALL

Jade Amenta (Melissa Jarrett) 1991

Jade is the daughter of film director Pino Amenta who made the film *Heaven Tonight* with former *Neighbours* star Guy Pearce. Melissa was Jade's first professional role which she started at the tender age of fourteen.

Jeremy Angerson (Josh Anderson) 1991–1992

Jeremy was actually eighteen when he landed the role of fourteen-year-old brainbox Josh. Originally from Adelaide, he moved in with co-star Richard Norton when he made the move to Melbourne to be in *Neighbours*.

Jeremy's big break came when an Australian film director spotted him selling hats at the Adelaide Grand Prix and offered him the lead role in *Sebastian and the Sparrow*, a film in which Jeremy played a street kid.

After leaving *Neighbours*, Jeremy came to the UK where he appeared in panto but struggled to find any other work. Eventually though, Jeremy landed a part in an Italian TV series.

Felice Arena (Marco Alessi) 1993

The eldest child of Italian immigrants, Felice may have become an Olympic swimmer; however, his flair for acting and singing took him away from his rural hometown of Bendigo in Victoria and led him to Melbourne. There he studied with former *Prisoner* star Betty Bobbit, among others. His big break came when he won a nation-wide competition for a guest role in *Neighbours* in 1990. A year later he appeared in *Neighbours* again as a guest at Melanie Pearson's engagement party. After that, Felice was the only Australian invited to join a United Nations touring musical, *Peace Child*, which took him to America and Ireland.

On his return to Australia, he called the *Neighbours* casting office who offered him the part of Marco.

Felice stayed in Ramsay Street for just six months before heading to the UK where he recorded a club single – a cover of the Bee Gees' 'More Than A Woman' – under the name of Moses. He promptly landed the role of Woof in the West End revival of *Hair*, and when that closed he took the lead in a national tour of *Godspell* – playing Jesus!

Lisa Armytage (Beverly Marshall) 1988–1989

British born Beverly has two children Rosita and Danika by her lawyer husband. After leaving *Neighbours* she appeared in TV commercials in Australia and bought a holiday home in Devon in the UK to be near her relatives in Bideford.

Elspeth Ballantyne (Cathy Alessi) 1993–1994

Elspeth became a cult heroine as prison officer Meg Morris in the Grundy soap *Prisoner*. After being the only actress to appear in all 692 episodes of *Prisoner*, Elspeth went on to do the kids' programme *The True Story of Spit McPhee* and worked extensively in theatre. She was tempted back into major soaps by the similarities between herself and Cathy Alessi. Like the character, Elspeth also has two teenage sons.

Troy Beckwith (Michael Martin) 1993 – present day

Unlike the menacing character he plays in *Neighbours*, Troy is in fact a mild-mannered dry-cleaning apprentice. This sensible lad decided to follow in the footsteps of his dad and have a trade behind him before launching into the precarious world of show-biz. He is the youngest of a large brood which includes five half-brothers and a sister. His ambition is to appear in a major block buster movie like *Jurassic Park*.

Troy actually made his first appearance in *Neighbours* a couple of years before he starred as Michael. He originally played another baddie, school-yard bully Darren Wood, who fought with Todd for Cody.

Francis Bell (Max Ramsay) 1986–1987

Prior to *Neighbours*, Francis had already become a familiar face on Australian TV from his appearances in *The Sullivans*, *Cop Shop* and *Carson's Law*.

After Neighbours, Francis returned to his home town in Auckland, New Zealand where he found full time acting work appearing in popular shows such as *Gold* and *Homeward Bound*, as well as commercials.

Francis had quite a reputation as an impressionist and could impersonate well-known people from Ray Charles to Prince Charles, and used this skill for voice-overs.

He was also a writer, director and singer and demonstrated all these talents when he toured his own production *Illuminatus* round the UK.

Sadly, his personal life could not match the success of his professional life and his childless marriage ended in divorce. Following the split Francis became depressed and checked himself into hospital for mental health treatment. However, he later checked himself out and in May 1994 committed suicide by jumping off a tower block in Auckland. He was 50.

Melissa Bell (Lucy Robinson) 1992–1993, 1994

Already familiar to the Australian viewing public as Janine in *E Street*, she returned to the Westside show after leaving Ramsay Street – as a completely different character called Bonnie! Melissa dated *E Street* producer Forrest Redlich's son Jason, and their liaison became public when he kissed and told about their relationship to the British press.

After *E Street*, Melissa came to Britain where she became great mates with *EastEnders* star Danniella Westbrook. After finding little work in London she returned to Australia to guest in the 2000th episode. She also filmed a pilot for a chat show which she hosted with *A Country Practice* star Matt Day called *Land Down Under*. Melissa later appeared in *Paradise Beach*.

Dasha Blahova (Maria Ramsay) 1986–1987

Since leaving *Neighbours*, Dasha – who has two children Maria and Oliver – has appeared consistently in theatre, even writing and directing some productions.

She also regularly appears on TV and has turned up in the soap *GP*. Dasha has also been the subject of a documentary by Czech TV called simply *Dasha* which chronicled her career in theatre which has taken her to many countries worldwide including France, Germany, England, Yugoslavia and Canada.

She emigrated to Australia from her native country Czechoslovakia in 1980 and appeared in *A Country Practice* (twice) and *Cop Shop* before being offered the part of Maria.

Although Dasha still bases herself in Australia, she regularly makes the trip to Prague where she has starred in several films. Naturally, such a well-travelled actress is good at languages. Dasha is fluent in Czech, English, Russian, French, Polish and Slovak!

Rachel was born in Borneo to an American father and Australian mother. But before the family, including her younger sister Ruth, settled in Australia, they lived in Canada, Spain, Scotland and the United States. Her father Harold intended to leave the oil business and buy a farm, but before that, the Blakelys decided to take a camping holiday. Rachel was twelve at the time, and she was about to grow up fast. Her mum Bronwyn was bitten by a mosquito carrying a tropical virus and she contracted the brain disease encephalitis. She was rushed to hospital but was dead within days.

Her dad went ahead with the plan to buy a farm and Rachel spent her teenage years on a remote cattle station taking school lessons by correspondence. When she got a summer job she had to swim across a river to get there because her farm was so isolated!

At eighteen, Rachel made the break and headed for the city where she started a successful career as a model after two friends entered her photo in a competition. When the *Neighbours* casting office spotted her on the cover of a magazine, they invited her to audition for the role of Gaby.

Rachel met her actor husband Peter Craig while helping out a friend on the door of a Melbourne nightclub, The Redhead. She wasn't going to let him in because he looked so scruffy, but he persisted and the two ended up going out on a date and they married when Rachel was 21.

Gayle and Gillian Blakeney (Christina and Caroline Alessi) 1990–1993

Born in Brisbane in 1966 these identical twins were destined for careers in showbusiness. They made their TV debut at the age of thirteen and have since made their mark in acting, singing and presenting. Already favourites Down Under from the kids show *Wombat*, Gayle and Gillian joined *Neighbours* in 1989 (but weren't seen on screen in Britain until the following year). They were signed by recording giants Stock, Aitken and Waterman, but their debut single 'All Mixed Up' only reached Number 74 in the charts.

Gayle's on-screen romance with Stefan Dennis' character Paul Robinson mirrored their liaison off-camera and the couple dated for almost three years.

The twins left *Neighbours* in Australia in 1992 and settled in London where they recorded more songs, this time with Mushroom records. Their single 'Mad If Ya Don't' disappeared without trace, and their follow-up, a cover of the Prince classic 'I Wanna Be Your Lover', went the same way.

Apart from regular panto appearances and PAs in nightclubs, work was thin on the ground for the twins who later landed the contract as the new 'Head 'n' Shoulders' celebrities and appeared in the TV ads for the shampoo.

Vikki Blanche (Julie Robinson) 1986–1987

Vikki left *Neighbours* to study acting in New York where she became a regular on the Greenwich

Village scene. She returned to Australia where she continued to appear on television in *The Flying Doctors* as Paula Patterson and as an undercover cop in the drama *Phoenix*.

Vikki – who dated co-star David Clencie while she was with the show – has not only been taking acting classes, but has recently been studying creative writing.

Ernie Bourne (Rob Lewis) 1988–1990

Ernie is a well-known actor in Australia who has appeared in guest roles in several other series. He also has a secondary career as a cabaret and musical comedy artist, and in 1994 took on a major role in the Australian revival of *Me and My Girl*.

Beth Buchanan (Gemma Ramsay) 1991–1992

It seems showbusiness was running through this talented actress's veins. Not only is she the younger sister of Simone Buchanan (from Oz TV's *Hey Dad*), but her brother Miles is also an actor. She appeared as Gemma for a little over a year and left with the intention of combining a career in acting with becoming a mature age student at university.

For a while she dated the Irish comedian Sean Hughes and also took a four-week contract to appear in *Paradise Beach* in 1994.

Joy Chambers (Rosemary Daniels) 1987 – present day (appears intermittently)

Joy is part of Australian TV royalty as she is the wife of Reg Grundy, head of the Grundy Organisation which makes *Neighbours* as well as *Sons and Daughters*, *Prisoner*, and *The Young Doctors*.

Joy met Reg when she was just eighteen and the couple have been devoted to each other ever since.

Before becoming popular as *Neighbours'* recurring character of Rosemary (every so often she darts in from New York to visit her mum Helen), Joy was already familiar to audiences from her regular role in *The Young Doctors*.

When she's not acting, Joy turns her attentions to her flourishing writing career following the successful publication in 1992 of her first novel, *Mayfield*.

She lives in Bermuda with Reg and their beloved dog Calpurnia.

Anne Charleston (Madge Mitchell/Ramsay/Bishop) 1987–1993

Anne only started taking drama lessons in a bid to improve her speech pattern! But she soon found she had a flair for acting and has never looked back.

After a varied career of stagework, modelling and small appearances in TV shows like *Prisoner*, Anne found international fame as brash Madge Mitchell. During her years with *Neighbours*, she made several trips to the UK for panto appearances, and when she left Erinsborough in 1993 Anne made her way to the British Isles once again to appear in a national tour of *The Cemetery Club*. She bought a house in a remote area of Galway in Ireland where she now lives alone.

She has a son Nicholas by David Ravenswood although the two never married. Following the tragic death of her cousin, Anne fostered her cousin's daughter Emma and brought her up as her own.

Anne – who has battled with and beaten breast cancer – is great friends with her *Neighbours* co-stars Ian Smith and Maggie Dence, and for many years remained a confidante of screen daughter Kylie Minogue as she embarked on her international singing career.

David Clencie (Danny Ramsay) 1986–1987

David was eased out of *Neighbours* when the show was taken over by Channel Ten after it was alleged that he was becoming difficult to work with. Still, *Neighbours* wasn't an entirely unpleasant experience for the young actor who met his then girlfriend Vikki Blanche on the set.

Already a familiar face from his appearance in *The Sullivans*, David went on to appear in *Cop Shop*. He later turned his back on acting almost entirely and carved out successful careers for himself in real estate and advertising.

Fiona Corke (Gail Lewis/Robinson) 1987–1989

Fiona left her country town home and headed for the city when she was just eighteen with the sole intention of becoming an actress. However, work wasn't that easy to come by and she went travelling, spending several months in Mexico.

Working in *Neighbours* was a joy for Fiona who had the chance to work with her boyfriend Nick Caraffa who turned up in the Coffee Shop as Tony Romeo. It also gave her the opportunity to travel to Britain when she was asked to appear in the Royal Variety Performance in 1990.

Fiona still works as an actress in Australia and recently appeared in a spy show called *Secrets* and the mini-series *The Man From Snowy River*.

Lucinda Cowden (Melanie Pearson) 1987–1992

Before appearing in *Neighbours*, Lucinda was previously in *Prisoner* and the ill-fated soap *The Power, The Passion*. She originally appeared as mad Melanie for seven episodes in 1987 as Henry's girlfriend. She begged the producers to return and in 1988 she returned for six episodes as Paul's temporary secretary. It wasn't until 1989 that Lucinda became a regular in Ramsay Street.

Lucinda married, but later separated from Aussie comedian David Cotter. She came to the UK to star in panto but also took on the lead in a touring production of *Peter Pan*. When that had finished she took over as presenter of the BBC children's show *Parallel 9* from former cast mate Richard Norton.

Lochie Daddo (Stephen Gottlieb) 1993–1994

Younger brother of the more famous Daddos, Cameron and Andrew (the Daddo brothers are more famous in Australia than the Minogue sisters!), this role in *Neighbours* gave Lochie (real name Christopher Lachlan Daddo) a chance to prove he was as good as his brothers. Lochie also has another brother, his twin Jamie, who was paralysed in an accident in 1987. Lochie therefore felt he had something special to add to his performance when Stephen was wheelchair-bound for a couple of months.

He stayed with the show for just a year and said he had been frustrated that Stephen rarely had a storyline away from wife Phoebe. On leaving Ramsay Street, surfer Lochie took a long holiday in Bali and on his return to Australia captured the headlines when he kissed another man as the gay lover of a doctor in the soap *GP*. In real life, Lochie can more commonly be found kissing his girlfriend, model Voni Delfos.

He seized the chance to finally play a baddie when *Paradise Beach* offered him the role of slimy Angel which lasted five weeks.

Alan Dale (Jim Robinson) 1986–1994

A native of New Zealand, Alan tried his hand at being a car salesman, a real estate agent and a milkman before he landed his first job in showbusiness. While he was doing his milk rounds one day he heard a DJ quit live on air. That afternoon he went to the radio station and asked them to give him the job – and they did! He also got a part in a TV show called Radio Waves.

In 1979, with just a few thousand dollars in his pocket, Alan moved to Australia in a bid to become a major radio DJ but within weeks had won the part of Dr Forrest in *The Young Doctors*, a role that would make him an international star.

His first marriage to his childhood sweetheart Claire foundered, and their two sons, Matthew and Simon, moved to live with their dad in Australia.

Remarkably, Alan was not the first choice to play neighbour Jim – he was only given the part after Robin Harrison turned down the offer at the last minute.

He met his second wife Tracy Pearson – a former Miss Australia – while indulging in his passion for sports cars at a charity motor racing event.

Since leaving Ramsay Street, Alan has taken singing lessons and concentrated on his career away from series television. He provides the voice-over for many ads in Australia, but did make one return to the small screen as a villain in the show *Time Tracks*.

Kimberley Davies (Annalise Hartman)
1993 – present day

Kim grew up on a farm in rural Victoria, moved to the city and became a successful model. While she was still at school, she wrote a play and went on to win the Australian Young Writers Award.

Before she joined the *Neighbours* cast she dated Scott Michaelson, but the two had already split up by the time she started playing man-eating Annalise. During her first year in *Neighbours* she shared a house with co-star Sarah Vandenbergh, but when Sarah left the show Kim rented a house by herself.

Maggie Dence (Dorothy Burke) 1991–1993

Already famous for playing Rose Sullivan in *The Sullivans* and Bev Baker in *Prisoner*, Maggie was a familiar face when she turned up in Ramsay Street.

She married her husband-turned-director Graham Rouse (who directed on *E Street*) in 1965, and although they never had kids they are devoted to their dog Ruth. Working in Melbourne away from their Sydney home was a big wrench for Maggie who had it written into her contract that she had every seventh week off!

After leaving *Neighbours*, Maggie made her way to Torquay in Devon to appear in pantomime with Melissa Bell.

Stefan Dennis (Paul Robinson) 1986–1993, 1994

Stefan trained as a chef before becoming an actor so he could always support himself if the acting work dried up. Stefan very nearly missed out on the part of Paul as he first auditioned for both Shane and Des! Before *Neighbours*, Stefan made several appearances as assorted criminals in *Cop Shop* and also turned up in *The Sullivans* and *The Young Doctors*. Stefan is also a singer and as a teenager formed a group with his brother Chris (his brother John was killed in a hit and run accident when Stefan was just nine). He later released a single, 'Don't It Make You Feel Good', which reached Number 16 in the UK charts. His follow-up single, 'This Love Affair', peaked at only Number 67.

He was married to wife Roz Roy for eleven years,

after which he dated co-star Gayle Blakeney for almost three years.

On leaving *Neighbours*, like many of his co-stars he headed for the UK during the panto season, but stayed on to play the lead in *Whose Life Is It Anyway?* portraying a disabled young man fighting for his right to die. Stefan returned to Australia and *Neighbours* to reprise his role of Paul for the 2000th episode.

Myra de Groot (Eileen Clarke) 1986–1988

One of Australia's most respected actresses, British born Myra had appeared in *The Sullivans* before terrorising Erinsborough as interfering gossip Eileen. She was adored by the younger cast, particularly Jason Donovan who dedicated his silver Logie to her in 1988 shortly before her death to cancer.

Jason Donovan (Scott Robinson) 1987–1990

Just about the most popular actor to ever appear in *Neighbours*, Jason quickly became the number one pin-up in both Britain and Australia. His career as a singer took off while he was still part of the *Neighbours* cast (see *Jason and Kylie – Singing Soap Stars*), and after he left the show his chart success went through the roof.

He also starred in the mini-series *Heroes*, but he didn't really confound his critics until 1992 when he took the West End by storm in *Joseph and His Amazing Technicolour Dreamcoat*, and proved conclusively that he could sing as well as act.

252

During his time in London he was subjected to much press intrusion – some of which insinuated that he was gay. However, it wasn't until *The Face* magazine printed an article in 1992 which Jason felt portrayed him as a hypocrite as it implied that he had lied about his sexuality, that Jason went to court to set the record straight. He wasn't gay – he was dating model Tara Owens – and he won the libel action.

After a break from playing Joseph, Jason returned to the role and continued with his pop career. In 1993, he spent some time in Queensland filming a movie called *Rough Diamonds*.

Before becoming a neighbour, Jason had worked in several TV shows – *I Can Jump Puddles*, *Golden Pennies* and *Skyways* with Kylie Minogue.

He is, of course, the son of Terry Donovan who brought Jason up single-handedly after breaking up with Jason's mum, newsreader Sue McIntosh.

Jason had little contact with his mum while he was growing up, but after he found fame in Ramsay Street, he re-established contact with her, and the two now see each other more regularly.

Terence Donovan (Doug Willis) 1991 – present day

Terry Donovan has a place in the Aussie Soap Hall of Fame! Apart from taking the credit for producing one of its greatest exports – his son Jason – Terry Donovan has appeared in so many shows it's hard to turn your TV on without catching him. He starred in the great Australian drama *The Man From Snowy River*, as well as TV shows such as *The Flying*

Doctors. Terry – as everyone calls him – also appeared in the British film *Oliver!*

He first made an impact on UK audiences as evil Al Simpson in *Home and Away*. He joined *Neighbours* in 1990 (although he wasn't seen in Britain until 1991) and hasn't looked back.

His first marriage to Sue McIntosh ended in divorce, but he has subsequently married Marlene with whom he has another son, Paul.

Dan Falzon (Rick Alessi) 1993 – present day

Dan is undoubtedly the current pin-up of *Neighbours* – and his good looks mean he is pestered wherever he goes. But his success hasn't gone to his head and Dan continued with his school studies between scenes. He took two years to complete his VCE (the Melbourne equivalent of A levels) so he graduated the same year as his younger brother, Tom.

Helping him keep his feet on the ground are his supportive Italian family with whom he still lives in Melbourne.

A keen athlete, Dan had been in the state hockey team for five years before joining the show, and he also plays cricket, soccer, swimming and tennis.

If his career in acting doesn't pan out, Dan says he'd like to pursue a career as a marine biologist or zoologist.

Kylie Flinker (Lucy Robinson) 1986–1988

This talented young actress left the soap when her school work load increased. She later concentrated on her studies but was occasionally seen on Australian TV – usually in commercials. In 1994, Kylie took a break from studies, acting and Australia to join a kibbutz in Israel.

Ally Fowler (Zoe Davies) 1987–1988

Alexandra Fowler was launched into the limelight from obscurity when she was nineteen. She had won the high profile part of Angela Hamilton in the hugely successful soap *Sons and Daughters*. Previously her only TV exposure had been a brief stint in *The Young Doctors*.

This success made her one of Australia's favourite actresses and she has worked steadily in theatre and small TV roles. After *Neighbours*, work was thin on the ground until she found a small role in *The Flying Doctors*. She later starred in the drama *Frankie's House*.

Amelia Frid (Cody Willis) 1990–1991

Amelia left *Neighbours* at the age of fifteen so she could concentrate on her schooling. She was great mates with Ian Williams who played her big brother Adam and the two stayed in touch after she left. Amelia combined her acting and schooling by making occasional guest roles in other productions.

Rachel Friend (Bronwyn Davies) 1989–1991

Although Rachel left acting behind when she quit *Neighbours*, she has remained in the headlines as Mrs Craig McLachlan. The couple met on the set and coincidentally ended up playing lovers. They had a long engagement (Rachel joked that they'd both be 50 before they actually got married) as their work schedules were so full they couldn't find time for a honeymoon. They eventually tied the knot in early 1993.

Rachel now works in Australia as a TV journalist for *The Midday Show*.

Vivean Gray (Mrs Mangel) 1987–1991

Playing the most hated woman on Australian TV finally took its toll on British born Vivean after years of abuse from the public. At one stage her garden was vandalised by people who couldn't tell her apart from her waspish character. It got to the stage that she hardly ventured from her home for fear of being abused by *Neighbours* 'fans'. This caused Vivean to leave the show in 1991.

She had made a habit out of playing busybodies – when she joined *Neighbours* she was already familiar to everybody as *The Sullivans'* awful Mrs Jessup. Vivean – who has never married – also appeared in *Prisoner*.

Vivean is now in semi-retirement and she concentrates on her hobbies of playing the piano, photography and looking after her cats.

Anne Haddy (Helen Daniels) 1986 – present day

Not only is Anne the only surviving original character on screen, but she has also proved herself a survivor in real life.

She was born an only child in Quorn in South Australia but left for the UK when she was 23. There she met her first husband Max Dimmit. The couple returned to Australia and had two children, Jane and Tony.

She achieved fame as housekeeper Rosie Andrews in *Sons and Daughters*, but although her professional career bloomed, she was plagued by health worries. Anne has survived a heart attack, four heart bypass operations, and stomach cancer.

She says her near death experiences have taught her to enjoy every day and her second marriage to James Condon (who played conniving Douglas Blake early on in *Neighbours*) as much as possible.

Linda Hartley (Kerry Bishop) 1990–1992

This talented actress and singer suffered from anorexia and bulimia in her teenage years, but overcame them and appeared in the Australian production of *Cats* for several years making use of her marvellous singing voice. It was during her run in *Cats* that she met her husband.

After *Neighbours* she made her way to the UK where she made occasional guest appearances on TV shows.

Richard Huggett (Glen Donnelly) 1992–1993

Already famous from his role in *E Street* as menacing Sonny Bennett, Richard took on a totally different guise as soft-hearted Glen.

His exposure in *Neighbours* meant the offers of theatre work flew in from the UK, and after a successful panto run, Richard toured the British Isles in the Australian play *Anzacs*.

Natalia Imbruglia (Beth Brennan) 1993–1994

The producers of *Neighbours* were so impressed with Natalie's guest appearance as abused Beth in their location shoot on the Gold Coast that they soon wrote her into the regular cast in Ramsay Street.

Natalie was just seventeen when she left her Italian immigrant family (one older sister and two younger sisters) behind in the New South Wales coastal town of Berkeley Vale to make the move to Melbourne and *Neighbours*.

She became great friends with co-star Sarah Vandenbergh who shared her interest in spiritual matters, particularly the calming influence of crystals.

On leaving *Neighbours*, Natalie appeared in panto in Britain and spent a few weeks doing publicity for the show in the UK. On her return she changed agents and embarked on the gruelling task of auditioning for new projects hoping to land a role in a film or mini-series.

258

Annie Jones (Jane Harris) 1988–1990

Although she is rarely seen on TV in Britain any more, Annie Jones is one of Australia's most successful TV actresses.

She came to *Neighbours* fresh from a stint in *Sons and Daughters*, and when she left Ramsay Street Annie went on to appear in another soap, *Chances*, playing the hairdresser, Paris.

Annie's other TV appearances include *The Flying Doctors*, the mini-series *Jackaroo*, and a sitcom called *The Newlyweds* in which she appeared alongside Cathy Godbold (Meg Bowman in *Home and Away*).

She appeared in the period drama *Snowy* about European immigrants, as it basically told the tale of her mother's life story. Annie's parents are Hungarian immigrants who fled to Australia due to hardship in Europe.

Annie was born Annika Jasko in Australia, but her dad changed the family's name to ease their integration into Australian society. But they did not forget their Hungarian roots – Annie still speaks fluent Hungarian (in fact she only started to learn English when she started school).

Annie is married to TV director Paul Moloney and they live in Melbourne.

Sue Jones (Pam Willis) 1991 – present day

As her name suggests, Sue is originally from Wales, the country she left when she was only four years old. Her family moved to a remote sugar cane farm in Queensland where she grew up.

Sue only started drama classes so that she could avoid PE! But she didn't take the option of becoming an actress seriously as no one from her town had ever done that before, so she trained as a dental nurse.

However, she kept up with the acting on a part-time basis until it was clear that she could earn her living at it.

Sue has appeared in *The Sullivans*, *The Flying Doctors*, *Boys From The Bush* and the police series *Skirts* as well as a brief role in *Neighbours* in 1988 as Peggy O'Hara. In 1988 she was also nominated for a prestigious Australian Film Industry award for her role in the film *Mullaway* with Nadine Garner.

Sue was the co-host of a children's radio show for five years but she has never had any children herself. She lives in Melbourne with her partner Peter, who is a graphic designer.

Paul Keane (Des Clarke) 1986–1991

As a kid, Paul always thought that he'd grow up to be a rugby player. But a serious collar-bone injury put paid to that dream.

So he turned to acting and when he landed the part of Des he had no idea that it would lead to such fame. Like most of the show's actors, Paul expected *Neighbours* to be an insignificant soap that would last a couple of years before he faded back into obscurity.

But unlike the rest of the cast, Paul found it hard to cope with the instant fame and attention in the streets. It has been reported that he turned to drugs, principally cocaine, to help him cope with the stress, but they only caused him more problems.

He left *Neighbours* in 1990 and his girlfriend Ellen helped him fight his addiction. Paul dropped out of acting and took part-time work as a labourer.

Paul is a gifted drummer, and during his time with the show formed a band called Suitably Rough with Alan Dale, Peter O'Brien and Elaine Smith. He now plays with a pub band in Australia.

T. S. Kong (Raymond Lim) 1994

T. S. moved to Australia from Asia in the early seventies and before *Neighbours* treated acting as only a part-time profession as he is also a hard working architect who happens to run a successful city pub in Melbourne! Oh yes, and he also has his own construction company.

Jonathon Sammy-Lee (Wayne Duncan) 1993–1994

Jonathon's father, nightclub impresario Sammy Lee, died when he was just eleven and during his *Neighbours* run, Jonathon changed his name to include his father's to stop constant confusion with another Australian actor who was also called Jonathon Lee.

It is ironic that Jonathon found fame as a schoolteacher as he was a right horror when he was at school. In fact, when he was offered the opportunity to travel to Nepal when he was fifteen, Jonathon's head master encouraged him to go!

He spent four months in the Himalayas and his

time there encouraged him to travel, and over the years Jonathon has done some pretty strange jobs – like being a pig farmer in Tahiti!

Jonathon, who is unmarried and has no children, left *Neighbours* after just a year to see a bit more of the world and tackle some more varied roles.

Mark Little (Joe Mangel) 1989–1992

Mark was already a well-known stand-up comic and respected actor (he won the Penguin Award in 1986 for his role in *The Flying Doctors*) in Australia by the time he found international fame as Ramsay Street's lovable Joe.

Like many of his co-stars, Mark made the trip to Britain when his *Neighbours* contract ended, but unlike his pals, Mark has made the move permanent. Together with his wife Cathy and sons Jasper and Angus, he has settled in the UK where he appears on TV twice a week as the co-host of the hugely popular morning show, *The Big Breakfast*.

Mark is no stranger to presenting as he had fronted both a kids' TV show (from which he was sacked for airing his personal views) and a music show, *Countdown Revolution*, in Australia.

Mark is still a regular on the comedy circuit and frequently tours with his successful one-man shows.

Craig McLachlan (Henry Ramsay) 1988–1991

Aside from Kylie Minogue and Jason Donovan, Craig is perhaps the next most famous neighbour having conquered the realms of music, film, theatre and TV.

Craig left *Neighbours* and soon turned up as free-thinking schoolteacher Grant Mitchell in *Home and Away*. But his musical career soon took him away from television when he had Top Twenty hits in the UK and Australia from his first album with his new band Check 1–2 (rather more palatable for the record bosses than the name of his first band – The Y Fronts!).

Craig appeared in the film drama *Missing Without Leave* in New Zealand and also played the lead in the mini-series *Heroes II*. His performances received good reviews from critics, but it was still clear that Craig was destined for the musical stage. First he toured Australia in the lead role of Frank N. Furter in *The Rocky Horror Picture Show*, then he took London's West End by surprise when he played Danny in the revival of *Grease* singing opposite Debbie Gibson.

Craig grew up in the coastal town of Shelley Beach where he was spotted by a Sydney talent scout in a high school play who introduced him to modelling. But the pretentious world of fashion didn't suit laugh-a-minute Craig who threw it in and returned to Shelley Beach where he took a variety of jobs. He even had a job as a bank clerk but quit his new employment after only nineteen days when it was alleged that he sabotaged the accounts system for his own amusement!

He was a skinny teenager, but was persuaded by his girlfriend Karen to take up weightlifting to beef him up a bit. Karen also suggested that he try acting again, which he did and again was spotted by a talent scout. This time *Neighbours* was beckoning and there was to be no looking back.

Craig married childhood sweetheart Karen, but they later drifted apart and divorced. Craig remarried in early 1993 when he wed his former *Neighbours* co-star Rachel Friend.

Scott Michaelson (Brad Willis) 1992–1994

Before Scott became familiar to fans as dopey Brad, he had already appeared in *Neighbours* – twice! The first time was back in 1985, when the show was still with Channel Seven, as an extra. He returned a year later and was given lines when he played an angry customer in the Coffee Shop.

A career in acting was by no means a dead cert for Scott who trained as an accountant. Like many other money professionals, Scott lost everything he owned in the stock-market crash of 1987 and he had to take a job as a labourer to pay off his debts. He also did the odd modelling assignment to make ends meet.

He returned to his accountancy degree but landed the part of Brad before he completed his studies. He became so well-loved as Brad that at one point rumours abounded in the Australian press that Brad and Mark Gottlieb would be given their own spin-off show.

Scott is well known to be a keen surfer, but his love of the sun and sea led him to a cancer scare and he had a mole removed from his chest.

He is very close to his brother Antony, and the two lads shared Scott's Melbourne house before he left town for a guest appearance in *Paradise Beach* prior to travelling to London where he set up home in early 1994.

When he joined *Neighbours*, Scott had been dating his future co-star Kimberley Davies and after he left it was reported that the two had become a couple once again. If his acting career ever dries up, Scott says he wouldn't mind setting up shop as an antique dealer!

Kylie Minogue (Charlene Mitchell/Robinson)
1987–1989

No other cast member has done so much since leaving *Neighbours* or so successfully cast away their soap star tag. Even before Charlene waved goodbye to Ramsay Street, Kylie was already well on her way to international stardom. Aside from her phenomenal singing successes (which are documented in the chapter 'Kylie and Jason'), she also made her mark in the film world with her feature debut *The Delinquents*.

In 1992, Kylie released her 'Greatest Hits' album indicating the end of her contract with the producers Stock, Aitken and Waterman, and she signed with the label de-Construction indicating a move to more 'credible' music.

Kylie's success and good looks have meant that she has never been out of the papers. Her private life has probably been more heavily featured than her professional life, and over the years she has been associated with not only Jason Donovan, but also model Zane O'Donnell and INXS singer Michael Hutchence.

Benjamin Mitchell (Cameron Hudson) 1993–1994

Ben originally appeared in *Neighbours* three years before he made his name as Cameron the lawyer, when he played Cameron's cousin Brad briefly (of course the part of Brad eventually went to Scott Michaelson).

Ben's other flirtations with fame came with the TV cop drama series *Skirts* and the mini-series *Bony*. When he made the film *Father* he met his future *Neighbours* co-star Simone Robertson. Ben and Simone fell deeply in love while working on *Neighbours* and the couple now live together in Melbourne.

Ben is also a keen musician and a member of the pub band Tin Canal.

Julie Mullins (Julie Martin) 1993 – present day

A committed member of Greenpeace, Julie Mullins shares very few characteristics with her manipulative screen persona. For starters, Julie Mullins is about ten years younger than Julie Martin – the make-up department cut her hair and put Julie in dark make-up to age her for the part.

And unlike the TV horror, Julie Mullins is an exceptionally nice woman! Other differences include the fact that Julie Mullins is not married and does not have children. In fact about the only thing the two women share is their Christian name!

Richard Norton (Ryan McLachlan) 1991–1992

This Adelaide lad hit the big time when he joined *Neighbours*. He was soon poached by rival soap *Home and Away* to play Simon Fitzgerald. Naturally his appearances in these two shows made him a very recognisable face in the UK, and Richard came to Britain to star in panto.

While he was in the country he met his girlfriend Hayley, and their romance survived the long distance separation when Richard returned Down Under.

In 1992, Richard's career took a change of direction when he became the presenter for BBC 1's madcap kids' show *Parallel 9*. In order to get the job Richard had to marry Hayley to gain the appropriate work papers, but sadly his days in the *Parallel 9* hot seat were short-lived and he was replaced by another former *Neighbours* actress, Lucinda Cowden.

Richard was shot in the chest when he was eleven by a pal with a shotgun. The bullet pellet came within millimetres of killing Richard after it pierced his lung and became lodged in his heart muscle. The doctors decided it was safer to leave the pellet where it was than perform open-heart surgery. And so Richard still has a bullet fragment lodged in his heart!

Peter O'Brien (Shane Ramsay) 1986–1988

Perhaps the first star that *Neighbours* produced, Peter was an enormously popular actor when the show started. He dated his co-star Elaine Smith for four years, but later in 1991 married another actress, Jo Riding, whom he met while touring in *The Wizard of Oz* in Britain.

Peter received very positive reviews for his portrayal of a holocaust survivor in *Shayna Maidel . . . My Lovely* in London's West End with Anita Dobson before returning to Australia to star in a string of TV shows.

After *Neighbours*, Peter has turned up as Sam Patterson in *The Flying Doctors* and currently stars as a lawyer in *The Law of The Land*. His British TV appearances include playing a serial killer in *Taggart*, and in *The Alexei Sayle Show*, Peter appeared in a spoof seventies Aussie soap!

Tom Oliver (Lou Carpenter) 1989, 1993 – present day

Born in Hampshire, Tom grew up wanting to be a jockey, but it soon became clear that he would be too tall and too heavy to pursue his dream. So he joined the merchant navy and on his third trip to Australia, Tom jumped ship and decided to stay.

For his first three years in the country he worked as a ranch hand (working on horseback, of course) on a cattle station the size of his home county. It was only when he travelled to the major cities that Tom started acting seriously. His showbiz work includes appearances on *Prisoner* and *ABBA, the Movie*.

Tom is unusual in *Neighbours* history in that he was invited back to play Lou Carpenter four years after appearing as a guest star (traditionally, these roles are quickly recast).

He lives in Melbourne with his wife and indulges,

when shooting schedules allow, in horse-riding and gardening.

Geoff Paine (Clive Gibbons) 1987–1988

Geoff was so popular as Ramsay Street's madcap medic Clive that a pilot was made for his own spin-off show called *City Hospital*, although it wasn't picked up by the TV networks.

When his *Neighbours* run came to an end, Geoff made the requisite trip to Britain to cash in on his fame, but returned to Australia with very few credits to his name. He has since been a regular on the Aussie comedy show *The Comedy Company* as well as the Down Under improvisation show *Theatre Sports*. He also appeared in the police drama *Phoenix*.

Geoff also has a very good singing voice and toured in the lead role in the Aussie revival of the hippy musical *Hair*. Even when he's not working, Geoff has his hands full as the father of twins!

Ashley Paske (Matt Robinson) 1991–1992

Ash grew up with his younger sister in the industrial town of Woolongong, to the south of Sydney where his English born mother looked after them.

As well as starring in *Neighbours*, Ashley has had parts in *Richmond Hill* (as Marty) and *A Country Practice* (as Adam Campbell). On leaving *Neighbours*, Ashley headed for the British stage, and as well as appearing in panto, he also toured in a production of *Mask For Murder*.

Guy Pearce (Mike Young) 1987–1990

Born in England, Guy emigrated to Australia as a child where he later became state bodybuilding champion. As well as his sporting and acting talents, Guy is also a gifted musician and writes songs and formed a band with some of his co-stars called Albie Wild and the Dayglos.

His musical and acting talents made him perfect for the stage and on leaving *Neighbours*, Guy toured in *Grease* for a year. He returned to TV to play David Croft in *Home and Away* and a rancher in *The Man From Snowy River*. Guy has also starred in several films: as Errol Flynn in *My Forgotten Man*, as a drag queen in *The Adventures of Priscilla, Queen of the Desert*.

Darius Perkins (Scott Robinson) 1986–1987

Before his role as Scott, Darius had appeared briefly in *Prisoner* but received little attention. So the sudden fame that came with *Neighbours'* popularity came as a shock to this young man and he gained a reputation for being difficult to work with. So when Channel Ten took over the show they didn't renew Darius's contract and recast Jason Donovan as Scott.

Darius had a hard time finding acting work after Ramsay Street and had to take work as a picture-framer to make ends meet. Eventually he landed a guest role in *The Flying Doctors* and went on to guest in *Home and Away* for five weeks as Gary Samuels.

Ian Rawlings (Philip Martin) 1993 – present day

South Australian born Ian got his big break in showbusiness when he was asked to be one of the house models on *Wheel of Fortune*. From there he was picked to play the evil and cunning Wayne Hamilton in *Sons and Daughters*.

He was originally contracted for three months as Wayne, but was so good he was hired for five and a half years! He married and started a family, and also became a partner in a Sydney beauty salon called Chatterleys which provided him with an income during the lean years after *Sons and Daughters*.

Eventually, Ian returned to TV in a new soap called *The Power, The Passion*, but when it was axed after just eight months, he needed to find an alternative source of income and became a salesman at a freight shipping firm.

Ian is still with *Neighbours* and he lives in Melbourne with his family.

Marnie Reece-Wilmore (Debbie Martin) 1993 – present day

Marnie was born in Sydney but moved to the small town of Orange when she was twelve, but she hated it there so much that the family moved back to the big smoke. She has two older sisters (who are models) and an older brother who is a cameraman. Marnie also has three step sisters and a step brother from her father's second marriage.

She first got the acting bug at age seven and studied it extensively at school and took several radio presenting courses out of hours. Marnie actually landed the part of Debbie by mistake after auditioning for something else for Grundy. She didn't get the part she went for, but was more than consoled by a major role in *Neighbours*!

Simone Robertson (Phoebe Bright/Gottlieb)
1992–1994

Phoebe was originally conceived as just a guest role to spice up the plots for Josh and Todd. But Phoebe spiced them up so successfully that she soon became a Ramsay Street regular.

Simone's previous acting credits include the film *Father*, and it was on the set of this movie that she first met Ben Mitchell. However, it wasn't until they started working together on *Neighbours* that they fell in love. They now live together in Melbourne.

Bruce Samazan (Mark Gottlieb) 1994 – present day

Madagascan born Bruce was a model before he landed the part that made him a star – dippy Constable Max Simmons in *E Street*. He was so popular as Max that he won a Silver Logie every year he was with the show.

E Street also had another pleasant side-effect for 24-year-old Bruce – his girlfriend Romy Meerkin. They met when Romy visited the studio to study the set design as part of her degree course.

Their relationship survived a tough test when Bruce started the role of Mark as it meant moving to Melbourne from Sydney. Romy took the plunge and moved with her man to the new city.

Bruce's other talents include presenting (he hosts an Australian country music show called *Stampede*) and music. In 1993 he released his first single, a rap record called 'One of a Kind', but Bruce was unhappy with his recording deal and his music career was put on hold.

Kristian Schmid (Todd Landers) 1988–1993

Born in Australia to an Austrian dad and Hungarian mum, Kristian spent his early years in the Victorian town of Geelong. His parents owned a clothing company so Kristian and his brothers Adam and Karl never had to spend their pocket money on new clothes!

As a kid, Kristian was a keen gymnast and won the Victoria State championships. Kristian's other skills include juggling and riding a unicycle!

Kristian's first professional job was in fact his role in *Neighbours*, and he took Todd from a geeky twelve-year-old to a mature young man in the five years he was with the show.

For years, Kristian was a panto regular in the UK and when his *Neighbours* run ended he came to Britain to set up home. He was quickly offered a job as a guest presenter on the popular kids' TV show *Going Live*, but the Immigration Department soon put a stop to that and refused to issue him with the correct work papers.

However, Kristian stayed in London taking on theatre roles (including Puck in *Midsummer Night's*

Dream) whenever he could get the appropriate work papers.

Kristian is very close to his family (especially his grandmother with whom he lived while filming *Neighbours*) and he still sees them regularly.

Elaine Smith (Daphne Lawrence-Clarke) 1986–1989

It was on the set of *Neighbours* that Elaine first met Peter O'Brien, the man she dated for four years.

Scots born Elaine reckons she only got the part of Daphne the Stripper because of her haircut! It seems the casting director was looking for something a little different, and when Elaine turned up for her audition with spiky hair it struck a bell and she was hired.

She left the show after two and a half years and it was at her request that the hugely popular character of Daphne was killed off, freeing her to take other roles.

Elaine has since appeared in the kids' show *Bay City* as well as the sequel to *The Flying Doctors*, a show called *RFDS* in which she played Dr Sissy Wetherall. Elaine also enjoys theatre and in 1994 she travelled to New Zealand where she starred opposite David Soul in the musical *Blood Brothers*.

Ian Smith (Harold Bishop) 1988–1992

An only child, Ian was bright and imaginative, and his quirky ways gained him the nickname 'The Professor' at school!

He soon channelled his artistic tendencies into

acting and writing, and went on to make a profession out of those talents. He came to prominence as Ted Douglas from The Department in *Prisoner*, the soap for which he was also a scriptwriter and associate producer.

Ian continued his dual role as actor and writer in *Neighbours*, although he found it hard to write for his own character, Harold.

It was against his wishes that Harold was written out, but when Ian was asked to take a salary cut to do the same job, he felt he had no choice but to go.

Ian has been married to his wife Gail for over 25 years, but the couple have never had any children.

George Spartels (Benito Alessi) 1993–1994

George became familiar to Australian viewers as one of the hosts of the kids' TV show *Playskool*. He was less of a children's favourite as disciplinarian Benito.

George is married to the actress Liz Alexander and they have two daughters, Alexandria and Octavia. George himself grew up without a father after his parents divorced. He lost touch with his Greek dad, Harry, for over 20 years, but tracked him down in 1983 and father and son had an emotional reunion in Greece only weeks before Harry's death.

Mark Stevens (Nick Page) 1989–1990

Young Mark first made a name for himself appearing on *Young Talent Time* with Dannii Minogue. He always hoped to follow in the musical footsteps of his idol John Farnham, and when he left *Neighbours* he set about getting himself a record deal. Although he achieved this aim, differences with the record company meant he never released a hit single.

Sarah Vandenbergh (Lauren Carpenter) 1993–1994

A native Sydneysider, Sarah made the move to Melbourne when she started *Neighbours*, and found a new flatmate in the shape of co-star Kimberley Davies.

Playing Lauren was Sarah's first major TV role as her previous career had concentrated on classical dancing. Sarah also has a good singing voice, and now that she has left *Neighbours* she would like to break into musical theatre.

Andrew Williams (Guy Carpenter) 1992

A gifted musician, Andy was heavily involved in the Aussie music scene before coming to prominence as Guy. The Welsh born actor quickly moved to rival soap *E Street* after leaving Ramsay Street playing Jack Brown. Andrew actually got a recording contract with *E Street*'s production company Westside, but when the show was axed, so was Andy's contract.

He later chanced his luck in Hollywood and came up trumps with a role in *Melrose Place*! On screen, Andrew has broken several hearts, but in real life he is engaged to his long-time girlfriend Melissa Thomas.

Ian was a veteran of several films and theatre productions before finding the limelight as Adam. He toured with a theatre company in America and played guitar in a band called The Innocent. He also appeared in the mini-series *Bony* with Cameron Daddo.

Ian grew up on a small farm near Brisbane with his sister Jane, but his ambitions soon took him further afield. His musical abilities made him a natural for the stage, and after leaving *Neighbours* toured in the Australian production of *Godspell* as well as *Grease* in Ireland.